GRACE AND TORAH

by

J. M. Myers

FORTRESS PRESS   Philadelphia

Library of Congress Catalog Card Number 74–26343

ISBN 0–8006–1099–7

4633J74   Printed in the United States of America   1–1099

To
The Winebrenner Theological Seminary
Findlay, Ohio
for the opportunity so graciously
offered to the author to participate
in a rich, spiritual repast.

Contents

Preface

With some augmentation, chapters I, II, and IV of this book represent lectures delivered at The Winebrenner Theological Seminary in 1973 under the auspices of The Dr. Gale Ritz Lectureship, and are published herewith by the kind permission of President W. T. Jackson.

The writer would be remiss if he did not express his profound appreciation for the invitation of Winebrenner Seminary to deliver the Ritz Lectures and for the gracious hospitality extended to him by the faculty, students, alumni, and friends of the institution during his brief sojourn on their campus, notably to President Jackson and Professor Oscar C. Shultz. It proved to be an experience that will long be cherished. It provided an opportunity for fellowship with a group of dedicated servants of the Lord and to observe firsthand the marvelous atmosphere of a small Seminary devoted to the Scriptures and their proclamation in the Church it serves. The Seminary is inevitably the focal center of any Church if it fulfills its true function of preparing persons for her many and varied ministries. Without a Seminary—a seedbed of ministers—no Church can long maintain its identity. Conversely, no Seminary can operate successfully without the wholehearted support of the Church and congregations it serves.

These chapters are not exhaustive treatments. The subjects dealt with seek only to offer a broad outline or overview of the general patterns of grace and torah in the Bible. Hopefully, some readers may be moved to carry further certain suggestions, or even present other viewpoints. One of the aims of this monograph has been to stimulate a "search of the Scriptures." If it motivates just one person to restudy the Bible in its own historical and theological context it will not have been produced in vain.

The reader should know that abbreviations used in this book are those customarily used in the *Journal of Biblical Literature*.

Mrs. Mary Miller, my secretary, deserves the highest commendation for deciphering and typing almost indecipherable manuscripts with hardly an error. Thanks are due also to the Reverend Norman A. Hjelm, Director and Senior Editor of the Fortress Press, for his readiness to consider publication of the materials offered in this little volume.

J. M. Myers

Gettysburg, Pa.

Introduction

Since the Reformation in the sixteenth century it has been customary to speak of "law and gospel." This was due largely to the time sequence of Old and New Testament which led to the equation of the Old Testament with law and the New Testament with gospel.[1] But a closer examination of the two great literary deposits reveals the fact that there is gospel in the Old Testament and law in the New Testament, and serious students of biblical theology can no longer be content with clichés that are at best half truths.

The burden of these chapters is to show that the basic pattern of grace and torah in that order is original and is maintained in the prophets and certain New Testament documents. That pattern appears to have been established in the exodus events and the Sinaitic covenant. Whatever may have been the actual historical situation, Israel believed that Yahweh's grace abounded for her in both events,[2] and ever after celebrated them. Prophets and Psalmists, as well as others, refer to them or presuppose them in their sermons and songs. It can be said without equivocation that the *whole* Bible is a book of the grace of God.[3] It begins with the gift of creation and ends with that of the new Jerusalem but in between grace upon grace is experienced and proclaimed.

1. Cf. M. Noth, *The Laws in the Pentateuch and Other Essays,* trans. D. R. Ap-Thomas (Edinburgh and London: Oliver and Boyd, 1966), pp. 2–6. Note his order: covenant and law, pp. 20 ff., and W. Zimmerli, *Die Weltlichkeit des Alten Testaments* (Göttingen: Vandenhoeck and Ruprecht, 1971).
2. See D. J. McCarthy's review article, "Berith in Old Testament History and Theology" in *Biblica* 53 (1972): 110–121. A review of Lothar Perlitt, *Bundestheologie im Alten Testament,* Wissenschaftliche Monographien zum Alten und Neuen Testament, 36 (Neukirchen-Vluyn: Neukirchner Verlag, 1969).
3. Cf. G. A. F. Knight, *Law and Grace* (London: SCM Press, 1962), ". . . the Gospel as it is contained in the Old and New Testaments that comprise our Bible" (p. 13 f.). There is, indeed, a sense in which the OT, especially in the Call of Abraham and the Exodus-Sinai episodes, portrays a conception of grace much less quid pro quo than does the NT. Cf. Ps. 51:18–19.

1

I

The Exodus and
the Covenant of Sinai

Though it does not materially affect our thesis, because of recent
trends in literary criticism the basic structure and type of the
materials that we are looking at must be taken into account. As
indicated by the title of this chapter, we shall be concerned
mainly with Exod. 1–23 which tells the story of Israel's oppression in Egypt, Moses' experience on Sinai, the events leading to
liberation, the trek toward the holy mountain, the crossing of the
Reed Sea, and the giving of the covenant at Sinai.

Most of the material apart from the Book of the Covenant,
belongs to the early sources,[1] though often they are incapable of
being identified in detail with confidence. There are several
extended sections of P material such as the genealogical references
in 1:1–5; the divine colloquy with Moses and the Levitical
genealogy in 6:2–30; and the description of the plagues (frogs,
sores, pestilence, hail, locusts, darkness, death of the firstborn) and
the passover ordinances in 8–12. But just because these traditions
stand in P does not necessarily make them late; it is now quite
apparent to the writer that much old material has been transmitted in so-called literary strata of much later date.

A. ISRAEL IN EGYPT

The story of Israel's sojourn in Egypt is too well known to
require detailed recitation here. The family of Jacob moved to
Egypt in the wake of Joseph's viziership, perhaps induced by pres-
sures of prolonged famine in the land.[2] According to Exod. 12:40
(P) the Israelites remained in Egypt 430 years. That was certainly
enough time for the development of conditions stated to exist in
Exod. 1:1 ff. The locale where they were domiciled was geo-

graphically restricted and, allowing for the prolific nature of the people, would by then have become rather crowded. Moreover, it was a fertile area where flocks and herds could increase and perhaps impinge upon wider and wider circles of the surrounding countryside. In any case, at the time of the approaching exodus when the history and purpose of Israel's entrance into Egypt had been forgotten, these intruders were seen as a menace to the security, and possibly economy, of the land. Their position, industry, and proliferation were a definite threat to Egypt in case of attempted foreign invasion from Western Asia. "Behold," said the Pharaoh to his people, "the Israelites have become too numerous and too strong for us; come, let us take precautions against them lest they become so numerous that in case of war they should join forces with our enemies and fight against us, and so escape from the land" (Exod. 1:9–10). Evidently the Egyptian authorities found themselves in a dilemma. On the one hand they feared an alliance of Israel with a possible invader and on the other they recognized their economic contribution and their buffer state situation.

So the Pharaoh and his officials resorted to two methods of population control. First they tried the method of corvée, forced labor, to hold population growth in check. But the harder the Hebrews labored the hardier they became and instead of decreasing the birth rate, hard labor actually accelerated it. ". . . the more they oppressed them, the more they multiplied and expanded" (Exod. 1:12). Then they attempted a kind of underhanded method in the hope of a more long range control. They summoned the midwives and requested them to strangle or drown all the male babies. The midwives, however, refused to cooperate because "they feared God"; they allowed the children to live. When the midwives were reproached for their recalcitrance they cleared themselves by reminding the authorities that Hebrew women were unlike Egyptian women, "but are like animals, in that they are delivered before the midwife reaches them" (Exod. 1:19). To judge from the remark in 2:23 ff., the Pharaoh died without achieving any success in his calculated plan to reduce the Israelite population to manageable proportions. Neither did the lot of the Hebrews improve. Indeed they kept groaning and crying for help. These were but the birth pains of grace, the first signs of Yahweh's move to deliver his people.

4

B. THE STORY OF MOSES

The next step was the rise of a deliverer who was himself both product and victim of the common oppression suffered by the people of whom he was one. Connected with the tribe of Levi— the priestly family—Moses was, somewhat like Isaac, a saved or spared sacrifice inasmuch as he was preserved by a providential act. More than deliverance from the sentence decreed by the Pharaoh for male children born to the Hebrews was involved. Being taken into custody by Pharaoh's daughter, as the story is told, encompassed nursing care and later support in the royal establishment. For the former period Moses was placed in the care of his mother, once more an indication of the hand of Yahweh. In the ancient world, children were nursed and trained in the family tradition by the mother for a period of three years, when they were weaned.[3] According to Hebrew tradition, the earliest lessons were learned from mothers. There is thus every indication that Jokebed, the wife of the Levite Amram, inculcated love of piety and tradition in her son before he went to the palace. He doubtless learned the traditions of the fathers and the promises to them which became the bulwark of his later life. When he took up residence at the court he was already deeply imbued with knowledge of the God of his people. In line with Egyptian practice, he was also instructed in the wisdom of Egypt (Acts 7:22). Just what he imbibed in the schools of Egypt is uncertain but it hardly differed from that normally experienced by youths of the same age and standing.[4] They were not handled too gently and certainly were subjected to a rigorous curriculum. To judge from the references in many Egyptian wisdom documents the chief method and incentive for learning was the cane. "Spare the rod and spoil the child" represents a true description of the way of Egyptian instruction. The education of Moses, then, was in two great traditions—that of Israel and that of Egypt—which was later to enable him to deal effectively with his own people and with their oppressors.

During his presence at Pharoah's court, he did not lose contact with his own people. The working capital of Egypt was located at Tanis (ca. 35 miles northeast of the old Hyksos capital of Avaris), in the Nile Delta under Ramses I, though Thebes remained as the religious and seasonal capital. If the royal court was at Tanis, at the northeast extremity of the Delta, Moses could easily have visited his people on occasion. It was important for Egypt that such a base of operation be maintained in view of the Hittite movements in Syria at the time. It also fits in well with the biblical reference to the Hebrews' labors in the building of the store-cities of Pithom and Raamses (Exod. 1:11). The greater the pressure from Asia the more feverish would be the defense activities in the most vulnerable areas. That fact may suggest why the Egyptian oppression of the Hebrews increased from time to time. The urgency of the situation demanded haste.

In the course of one of his visits to a building site, Moses saw an Egyptian taskmaster beat a Hebrew slave to death. He took matters into his own hands and slew the taskmaster. He thought his act of violence went undetected. But on another occasion when he attempted to mediate between two of his own brethren, Moses was made painfully aware of the fact that someone had witnessed his deed. Even the Pharaoh knew about it and tried to do away with Moses. In the course of flight, Moses came to Midian where he agreed to reside with a priest whose daughter Zipporah he subsequently married.

Here, one day while tending his father-in-law's sheep, he met the God of the fathers about whom his mother must have told him. Perhaps it marked the surfacing of that early faith, which lay more or less dormant over the years, that now claimed his full allegiance. At any rate this experience signaled the beginning of a new phase of his education in further preparation for his mission as the mediator of God's grace to his ever more suffering and oppressed people. However one may interpret the external phenomena, the Sinai experience of Moses was fraught with meaning for him. Several factors may be noted as the story now stands —i.e., as tradition has transmitted it to us. (All of Exod. 3 belongs to the oldest strata.) The phenomenon of the burning bush had no other function than that of attracting the attention of the shepherd. The real thing was the voice that spoke to him. The double use of the name—Moses, Moses—points to the seriousness of the encounter between the refugee from Egypt and Yahweh who announced, "I am the God of your father, the God of Abraham, Isaac and Jacob" (3:6). Had Moses perhaps been thinking out there in the silent loneliness of the endless desert about what his mother taught him and about his brothers still smarting under the heavy yoke of oppression? It is rather striking that precisely those points constitute the word of the Lord to him at the moment. "I am the God of your father. . . . I have indeed seen the plight of my people who are in Egypt, and I have heard their cry under their oppressors; for I know their sorrows . . ." (Exod. 3:6–7). Moses may even have been contemplating the possibility of a rescue mission in view of the fact that the Pharaoh who knew about his murder of the Egyptian taskmaster was dead (Exod. 2:23). The Lord has a way of turning the deepest thoughts of men's minds into words of action! In a word, Moses faced the gravest crisis of his life. He was face to face with God and with himself. It was, I suppose, what psychologists would call an identity crises, but couched in terms of ancient Semitic thought patterns.

The voice from the bush appealed to Moses: "Come now, let me send you to Pharaoh to bring my people, the sons of Israel out of Egypt" (3:10). So overwhelming was the thought that he began to cringe. Unmindful of the long period of preparation, Moses cried, "Who am I that I should go to Pharaoh and that I should bring out the sons of Israel from Egypt" (3:11)? Moreover, "suppose I should go to the sons of Israel and tell them 'the God of your fathers has sent me to you,' and they say to me, 'What is his name?' What am I to say to them?" (3:13). Then, what "if they do not believe me and do not listen to me, and say 'Yahweh did not appear to you'" (4:1). A last desperate argument centered about his deficiency as a speaker (*lo' 'iš d^ebārîm 'anōki*) because (*k^ebad-peh w k^ebad lašōn 'anōki* = I am slow of speech and slow of tongue) (4:10). These protestations remind us of Jeremiah who pled that he was too young, too inexperienced, as a speaker for the Lord.

Nevertheless Yahweh's determination to save his people, to exercise his grace in their behalf was not to be deflected. Moses was informed that he would not have to go on his mission alone—*ki 'ehyeh 'immāk* (for I am with you) (3:12). So ineffable was the divine response that its success was guaranteed: "And this is the sign for you that I have sent you. When you bring the people out of Egypt, you shall worship God on this mountain" (3:12). To the second of Moses' caveats Yahweh responded by revealing to him his name. In answer to the third supposition raised by Moses, Yahweh gave him the sign of the staff-serpent (4:2 ff.). The reply to the pretext that he was not a good speaker was Yahweh's provision of Aaron who is characterized as a ready speaker (*ki dabber y*^{e} *dabber hu'*) (4:14).

All of the Sinai experience of Moses portrays the resolute will of Yahweh to effectuate his grace for the deliverance of his people from their otherwise hopeless condition. Up to this point that grace had, of course, not yet eventuated, though the promise was sure. One can hardly help seeing the operation of grace in the life of the leader as well as in the events encompassing the Israelite community.

C. EVENTS LEADING TO THE EXODUS

Reluctantly and with all sorts of misgivings, Moses, with his wife and sons, set out for Egypt. On the way, or perhaps before, Aaron, his brother, was sent to meet him. At the mountain of God, Moses apprized him of what Yahweh had told him about his plan to deliver Israel from slavery and bondage, and that he had been designated as his agent. Apparently Aaron agreed to serve, with his brother, in the capacity of speaker.

The initial contact was with the elders of Israel who, after hearing about the word of Yahweh and witnessing the signs performed by Moses and Aaron, agreed to cooperate, without, according to the scriptural story, too much difficulty. The most telling aspect of their task proved to be another matter. Feeling more sure of themselves now, they proceeded to present their case to the Pharaoh who immediately retorted, "Who is Yahweh that I should listen to him and send Israel away? I do not know Yahweh and I will not send Israel away" (5:2). Pressed further he accused the messengers of subverting the people inasmuch as they were interfering with their work. Meanwhile the Pharaoh sent word to the taskmasters to increase the workload of the Hebrew subjects so that they would have less time to ponder their lot and nurse discontent. Naturally the already overburdened slaves did not relish the increment of work thus laid upon them and turned against their would-be liberators. Meeting Moses and Aaron they remonstrated bitterly with them. "May Yahweh look upon and judge you because you have made us stink in the sight of Pharaoh and his servants, so as to put a sword in their hands to kill us" (5:21). Once more Moses complained to Yahweh because the affair turned out just as he expected. "O Lord why have you brought evil on this people? Why did you send me? Ever since I approached Pharaoh to speak in your name, he has ill-treated this people while you have done nothing to deliver your people" (5:22 f.).

The road from slavery to freedom is always long and hard, but Yahweh's grace and power are sufficient to do what he has willed. "Now see what I am about to do to Pharaoh; for with a mighty hand he will send them out, yes with a mighty hand he will drive them out from his land" (6:1[JE]). The first attempt of Moses and Aaron failed and had the repercussions already referred to. But Yahweh had only just begun to exert his power as demonstrated by the ten plagues.[5] Each appeal to Pharaoh was accompanied by an act, a kind of visible word of authority attributed to Yahweh with the intention of demonstrating his power. The Pharaoh was impressed but, as time went on, he became increasingly determined to hold on to the valuable source of labor essential for his purposes. The danger of revolt in connection with a possible foreign invasion had apparently subsided so that we hear no more about the plan of a former ruler to curb the population expansion. In fact, the plague narrative gives every impression of having been transmitted orally, its main purpose being to rehearse the mighty acts of God performed on behalf of his people by humiliating the greatest world empire of the period. It is a lesson repeated by the Psalmist:

> Argue, Yahweh, with my opponents,
> Fight against those who contend with me.
> Take shield and buckler,
> Rise up for my help.
> Take hold of spear and battle-axe to meet my pursuers;
> Say to me, "I am your salvation" (Ps. 35:1).

One must be careful, however, to note that Yahweh intervened only when the enemies of his people would otherwise have been insuperable.

The focus of the plague section is on the death of the firstborn of Egypt, the final blow against the oppressor of Israel. Most of the plague story belongs to the latest stratum of the Tetrateuch (P) whose main interest was in the ritual aspects of Israel's life and worship. The Hebrews were not directly involved in any of the plague events except the last one. The narrator expressly says four times that Israel (in the land of Goshen) was exempt from plagues. In connection with the last one, the people of Israel were cautioned to carry out a particular ritual that would cause the destroying angel to pass over their homes and leave the first-born untouched. The directions for avoiding the fate of Egyptian households belongs to the oldest source (L or J[1]). Every family was to slay a passover sacrifice and smear the lintel and doorposts with its blood; when the angel saw it he would pass over the house and let the firstborn live. This was to be a perpetual rite. "You shall observe this rite as an institution for all time, for you and your descendants. And when you enter the land which Yahweh will give you, as he promised, you shall observe this rite. And when your children ask you, 'what do you mean by this rite?' you shall say, 'It is the passover sacrifice to Yahweh, because he passed over the houses of the sons of Israel in Egypt when he struck down the Egyptians, but saved our houses'" (Exod. 12:24–27 [L]).[6] This was to be a commemorative celebration recalling God's gracious act of salvation.

D. THE EXODUS FROM EGYPT TO SINAI

Deliverance from Egypt, including the preparatory events, was Yahweh's doing and was marvellous in the sight of the people. The narrative begins with the final, terrible thrust against Egypt, and the sparing of Israel's firstborn. Pharaoh's firstborn was smitten as well as those of his subjects, producing the most pathetic, countrywide outcry ever heard in the land. Moses and Aaron were summoned in the middle of the night and urged to get the erstwhile Hebrew slaves out of Egypt, together with their children and their flocks. The hastening of the process now amounted to expulsion and was accentuated by overt pressure from every Egyptian family into whose midst Yahweh's angel of death had come. "The Egyptians urged the people on, to make them leave hastily, for they said, 'We shall all be dead'" (12:33).

Moses was careful not to direct the people along the nearest route to the promised land lest they be attacked by the border brigands and, being forced to fight become discouraged and want to return to Egypt. They would have to learn gradually that the way of freedom is often more difficult and trying than that of bondage. Yahweh himself took on the task of leading them by means of the pillar of cloud and fire (13:21 f.). He took them the long way around, as it were, because he was not yet done with Egypt and the obdurate Pharaoh. No sooner were the mourning rites over than news reached the court that Israel had departed. Then Pharaoh and his courtiers had second thoughts. "What have we done? We have sent away Israel from our service" (Exod. 14:5 [J]). At once they gathered their horses and chariots in full strength and set out in pursuit of fleeing Israel. Little did they know that their obduracy was to get them into further trouble with the all-powerful God of the fathers. A mobile army moving posthaste in pursuit soon overtook the motley concourse of people impeded by the presence of flocks, herds, women, and children.

The literary art of the redactors is superb. They have lingered on each of the stages of the exodus story with almost studied determination to portray the grandeur and glory of Yahweh contending with an obdurate king who thinks he is God, in behalf of a half-believing people whom he had chosen to be his very own, dedicated to his service for mankind. Thus it is that the plagues have been set in a schematic framework to show how Yahweh intervened for the deliverance of his people at different levels of their experience. What a majestic and lively portrait is sketched in Exod. 14! The people were deliberately led into a trap—"Tell the sons of Israel to turn back and encamp opposite Pi-hahiroth between Migdol and the sea" (14:2)—with a twofold purpose: the one to demonstrate Yahweh's power as measured against that of the mighty host of Egypt, the other to impress upon the people the limitless character of his saving grace.

The most celebrated episode of the whole narrative of the exodus is that of Israel's deliverance at the Reed Sea. Apart from its magnificent literary art, Exod. 15 breathes a spirit of thanksgiving for Yahweh's triumph over the Pharaoh and his army resulting in his final heroic act of grace for the salvation of Israel from the house of slaves. It is a confessional hymn of the victory (salvation) celebrating Yahweh's mighty act of grace.

> I will sing to Yahweh, for he has triumphed gloriously;
> Horse and rider he has tossed into the sea.
> Yahweh is my strength and my defense;[7]
> He has become my salvation.
> This is my God and I will enshrine[8] him,
> The God of my father and I will exalt him.
> Yahweh, the man of war—
> Yahweh is his name.
> Pharaoh's chariots and army
> He has thrown into the sea;

His select officers are drowned in Yam Suph.
The deeps covered [them],
They sank into the depths like a stone.
Your right hand, Yahweh, is powerful;
Your right hand, Yahweh, smashes the enemy.
In your great majesty you overthrow your foes;
You send forth your fury that consumes them like stubble.
At the blast of your nostrils the waters were heaped up;
The floods stood upright like a wall;
The deeps congealed in the midst of the sea.

The enemy said,
I will pursue, I will overtake,
I will apportion the booty;
My appetite will be satisfied.
I will bare my sword;
My hand shall vanquish.

You blew with your breath, the sea covered them;
Like lead they sank beneath the fearful waters.

Who is like you, Yahweh, among the mighty;
Who is like you, feared among the saints,
Revered for praiseworthy deeds, doer of wonders!

You stretched out your right hand,
The earth swallowed them.

By your *hesed* you led the people whom you redeemed;
By your might you guided them to your holy abode.
. . . .
When your people cross over, Yahweh,
When the people you created cross over,
You will bring them and plant them on the mountain of
    your heritage,
The dais of your throne that you, Yahweh, made,
The sanctuary, Yahweh, your hands established.
Yahweh will be king forever and ever! (Exod. 15:1–13, 16b–18).

The impression made by Yahweh's deliverance at the Reed Sea never faded from Israel's memory. It became as central to her faith as the crucifixion has been for Christians. In fact it was woven into many of her songs and liturgies. Only a few of them[9] can be mentioned here. There is the prophetic psalm, 76:7 (Heb.):

At your rebuke, O God of Jacob,
Chariot and horse were overcome.

The hymn composed of Ps. 77:14 unmistakably recalls the exodus event.

> You are the God who performs wonders;
> You have made known among the peoples your might.
> You have redeemed your people with your arm,
> O sons of Jacob and Joseph.

The same is true of the epic poem, 78:12–16:

> Before their fathers you performed wonders,
> In the land of Egypt, in the fields of Zoan.
> He cleft the sea and led them through:
> He made the waters stand like a heap.
> He led them with a cloud by day,
> And all through the night with light of fire.
> He split rocks in the desert,
> And gave them drink abundantly as from great depths.
> And he brought forth streams from the rock,
> And made water run down like rivers.

The cultic hymn Ps 105—is even more pointed.

> He greatly multiplied his people,
> And made them more numerous than their oppressors.
> He altered their heart so that they hated his people,
> So that they dealt deceptively with his servants.
> Then he sent Moses, his servant,
> And Aaron whom he had chosen.
> They wrought marvellous signs among them,
> And wonders in the land of Ham (vv. 24–27).

In the liturgical piece recited at the cult festival of the covenant community of Israel is this reference:

> He it was who smote the first-born of Egypt, both man and beast.
> He performed signs and wonders in your midst, O Egypt,
> Upon Pharaoh and all his servants (Ps. 135:8–9).

But perhaps most significant of all is the "Great Hallel," Ps. 136, whose linguistic form is late though its content is not. It may have been a harvest song celebrating the divine revelation of salvation in creation and history.[10] One might call it a *hesed* Psalm since the antiphonal response *ki l^e 'ōlām hasdo* for his *hesed* is eternal) occurs twenty-six times and since *hesed* is a covenantal term.

13

Give thanks—
To him who smote the Egyptians in their first-born—for his
    ḥesed is eternal;
And brought out Israel from their midst—for his *ḥesed* is eternal;
With a mighty hand and an outstretched arm—for his *ḥesed*
    is eternal;
To him who cut in two parts the Yam Suph—for his *ḥesed*
    is eternal;
And caused Israel to pass through its midst—for his *ḥesed*
    is eternal;
And shook off Pharaoh and his host in Yam Suph—for his *ḥesed*
    is eternal (10–15).

But Yahweh's acts of grace did not cease with destruction of the Pharaoh and his charioteers in the Reed Sea. Despite the peoples' complaints and disobedience he continued to shower them with his blessings. For three days they journeyed in the desert without water and when they came to Marah where there was a spring they could not drink the water because it was bitter. Then Yahweh showed Moses a tree whose branches when thrown into the water sweetened it and made it potable (15:22–26). At Elim they found twelve springs of water surrounded with palm trees (15:27). Some days later they ran out of food and cried for a return to the fleshpots of Egypt. Then Yahweh provided quail in the evening and manna in the morning—flesh and bread from heaven (16:13 ff.). Taking up their journey again they arrived at Rephidim (17:1 ff.) where there was no water. Once again Yahweh brought water for them from the rock at Massah-Meribah. Here for the first time they were opposed by Amalek (17:8 ff.) whom Joshua and his select warriors put to flight. Thus by the benevolence of Yahweh, Israel survived until Sinai was reached "on the third new moon after leaving the land of Egypt" (19:1).

E. THE COVENANT AT SINAI

No matter how one views the developmental situation surrounding the various legal codes of the Old Testament, or even the covenant pattern or formulary, it is perfectly clear that the tradition regarded the deliverance from Egypt as antecedent to the giving of the torah.[11] Yahweh established himself as the God of Israel by his saving acts; only then would he be in a position to lay down principles by which the community might be guided and maintain itself in covenant relationship with him. The

14

formula preserved in P's account of Yahweh's charge to Moses which the latter was to deliver to Israel is basic—"I am Yahweh; I will bring you out from under the burdens of Egypt and deliver you from their bondage. I will redeem you with an outstretched arm and by mighty judgments. And I will take you to myself for a people and I will be to you for God, so that you will know that I am Yahweh your God who has taken you out from under the burdens of Egypt. I will bring you unto the land which I swore to Abraham, Isaac, and Jacob and give it to you as a possession, I, Yahweh" (Exod. 6:6–8). Note the formula, "I will be to you for God and you shall be to me for people" which harks back to Gen. 17:7–8 (P) and becomes standard in later literature.[12]

By his mighty acts Yahweh had now shown himself without doubt to be God and the people had demonstrated their willingness to be called his people by the simple fact that they accepted his deliverance from bondage, from the power of the Pharaoh at the Reed Sea, drank the water he provided, and ate his quail and manna. That appears to have been the only quid pro quo. Yahweh had freely chosen Israel—as the Deuteronomist says, "not because you were the greatest of all the peoples, for you were the smallest of all peoples, but because Yahweh loved you . . ." (Deut. 7:7 f.).[13] And Israel chose to accept his intervention on their behalf. To free her from political and economic slavery at the time required an act of God. But to remain freedmen not subject to selfishness, greed, and passion demanded covenant with the God of their salvation.

At Sinai, according to tradition, Yahweh entered into that covenant relationship with his chosen people. The basic agreement was, of course, the so-called Decalogue which, as Albrecht Alt says, "refrains from naming actual individual cases, but tends rather to lay down principles, without getting lost, however, in abstractions."[14] G. E. Mendenhall,[15] K. Baltzer,[16] and others have shown that the covenant formulary reflects the Hittite suzerainty treaties. Those treaties begin with a recitation of the antecedant history that called forth the subsequent stipulations. The one coming closest to the Mosaic covenant is that between Suppiluliumas and Niqmadu of Ugarit where the former delivered the latter from a coalition of kings that threatened to destroy him and his people. The enslaved Hebrews too are said to have cried out by virtue of their oppression by Egypt. Yahweh heard their cry and sent a deliverer. Hence the preamble to the Decalogue, "I am Yahweh your God who brought you up out of the land of Egypt, out of the house of slaves" (Exod. 20:2; Deut, 5:6). Elsewhere there is frequent reference to the promise made to the fathers, notably to Abraham (Gen. 12), but not here; evidently the exodus covenant is based on immediately preceding historical events.

The code represents the principles for the people's relationship with Yahweh and with one another as his people. As such it was just as much an act of grace as the deliverance itself "by predicating the law upon God, who out of his goodness redeemed Israel from slavery (19:4–5; Hos. 13:4), the law becomes the instrument of a mutual relationship in which faith responds to love. This transforms the law into a form for expressing gratitude. The law, as the outcome of the covenant relationship, is thus itself a form of grace," writes J. C. Rylaarsdam.[17] The gift of torah was not for the purpose of Israel's salvation which had already been achieved by Yahweh in his victory over Egypt and the decimation of the Pharaoh and his host at the Reed Sea. It was for the maintenance of their relationship with him. How were they to respond to him who had so signally delivered them from bondage and slavery, even death, at the hands of the Egyptians? Because Yahweh had thus acted—and they had responded rather freely thereto—they were now his people more than ever. It was not just because of a promise to the fathers but by virtue of a saving act which they themselves had experienced. The torah is thus a guideline for those who had been covenanted by Yahweh.

As Yahweh's people henceforth, in a way not hitherto known, their eyes turned to him for further direction. What was his will for them now? How could their status as his people be maintained? How could they remain his people? Thus this further gracious act of torah (instruction) was imperative. Broad principles were laid down in the so-called "words" upon which all further relationships in the covenanted community were based. Israel was given the utmost freedom within the covenant stipulations resting on their acceptance of Yahweh's gift of deliverance. There is some difference of opinion as to whether "these words" ought to be interpreted as absolute imperatives or as indicatives. A. Weiser observes, "The fact that the commandments of the Decalogue are formulated in the indicative still points to Yahweh's announcement of his will belonging to and corresponding with that of his nature; in this form it is the divine proclamation of the *nature* of God's people who are set in contrast to their surroundings by the negative way of expressing prohibitions."[18] That is precisely it. The freed people were not (and would not be) dwelling in a realm isolated from the rest of the world.[19] They were in the midst of a very different and increasingly tempting world. But they were Yahweh's people in that world. "These words," then, were the declaration of his will without threats or punishments.

> You will have no other gods beside me.
> You will not sculpture an image for yourself.
> You will not attribute to me what I did not have in mind.
> Remember the Sabbath Day.[20]
> Honor your father and mother.
> You will do no murder.
> You will not commit adultery.
> You will not steal.
> You will not bear false witness.
> You will not covet.

There was obviously some development in "these words" as has been observed by scholars for a long time, but the basic elements of Yahweh's will must have been something like that.

Deliverance and covenant belong together. Both are acts of divine grace. What developed later in line with "these words" and which is known as the torah was nothing more or less than an application of these principles to situational exigencies. The broadest meaning of torah is instruction, teaching, and not law in our sense of the term. It is divine guidance for a supposedly commited people and ought to be recognized as such. It is the repertoire of God's gracious will for a people who had accepted his prior gift and in appreciation therefor placed themselves under his tutelage. Response to torah is an act of gratitude. Failure to do so is an affront to covenant and a tacit rejection of Yahweh's grace.

CONCLUSION

Viewed from the standpoint oultined above, the idea of grace and torah takes on a much greater significance than is usually recognized. Israel's sorry state in Egypt as related in the first chapters of Exodus represents a condition of utter hopelessness from a human point of view. It could be alleviated only by the direct intervention of Yahweh who was moved by the plaintive cry of the sons of Israel for deliverance. He prepared an intermediary through a long period of education. But he also acted himself in support of his servant Moses in many wonderful ways—many of them by intensification of natural phenomena. He intervened to provide release from Egyptian enslavement, for food and water in the desert, for the defeat of the Pharaoh and his host at the Reed Sea, and for that of Amalek.

For the confirmation and furtherance of his deliverance, Yahweh entered into a covenant with his freed people. He revealed to them directly—"God spoke all these words" (Exod. 20)—his will for them by an announcement of principles by which they could remain free and his forever. Perhaps Israel's creed is best expressed in Deut. 26:5b–9: "My father was a fugitive Aramean. He went down to Egypt and sojourned there, few in number; there he became a nation, great, powerful, and populous. And the Egyptians treated us harshly, and afflicted us, and put us under severe bondage. Then we cried to Yahweh, the God of our fathers, and Yahweh listened to our voice, and saw our sorry plight, our hard labor, and our oppression. So Yahweh brought us out of Egypt with a mighty hand and an outstretched arm, with great terror, and with signs and wonders; he brought us unto this place and gave us this land, a land flowing with milk and honey."[21]

NOTES

1. Following O. Eissfeldt's analysis in *The Old Testament: An Introduction* (New York: Harper and Row, 1965) [asterisks indicate that this passage may include material shared by another source as well]:

L	J	E	P
1–2*	1–2*	1–2*	1:1–5,7*,13, 14*
3:21–22	3*	3*	2:23a, b–25
4:1–9,19–26,30b–31a	4:18, 29, 31b	4:10–17,	6:2–30
7:15b, 17b, 20a, b	5*	27–28,30a	7:1–13;19–20aa,
12:21–27,33–39	6:1*	5*	21b–22
13:3–16*, 20	7–9*	6:1*	8:1–3, 11b–15
14*	12:29–30, 32	7–11*	9:8–12; 12:20, 28
15:20–27	13:21–22	12:31	12:40–13:2
16*	14*	13:17–19	16:1*,2–3,
17:1a,8–16	16*	14*	6–13a,14*
19:2–25*	17:1b–7*	17:1b–7*	19:1
	18*	18*	
	19:2–25*	19:2–25*	
	20:18*, 20*	20:18*,19,	
	23:20–33*	20*	
		21:1–17	
		23:20–33*	

2. Anastasi Papyrus IV records the passage of Edomites through the fortresses of Merneptah Hotep-hir-Maat in the thirteenth cent. B.C. (Pritchard, *ANET*, p. 259).

3. A. Erman, *Life in Ancient Egypt*, trans. H. M. Tirard, (London: Macmillan, 1894), p. 163; A Bertholet, *A History of Hebrew Civilization*, trans. A. K. Dallas (New York: Brentano, 1926), p. 162.

4. Cf. Erman, *op. cit.*, chap. 14; John A. Wilson, *The Burden of Egypt* (Chicago: University of Chicago Press, 1951), pp. 225 ff.

5. On the plagues see the commentaries and Greta Hort, "The Plagues of Egypt," *ZAW* 69 (1957); 84–103; 70 (1958): 49–59. However one may interpret the plagues themselves, they were certainly regarded by the writer as wonders, miracles, performed to impress the Pharaoh with the mighty power of Yahweh. Perhaps part of the miraculous element consisted in the intensity of natural phenomena coinciding with negotiations of Moses and Aaron. For a discussion of the plague narrative with its literary problems, see M. Noth, *Exodus* (Philadelphia: Westminster Press, 1962); pp. 67–71 and Moshe Greenberg, "The Redaction of the Plague Narrative in Exodus" in *Near Eastern Studies in Honor of William Foxwell Albright*, ed. Hans Goedicke (Baltimore: The Johns Hopkins Press, 1971), pp. 243–252.

6. Cf. Greenberg, *ibid.*, p. 279 f.

7. See Frank M. Cross, Jr., and David Noel Freedman, "The Song of Miriam" in *JNES*, 14 (1955): 243, n. b.

8. *Ibid.*, p. 244 and H. M. Orlinsky, *Notes on the New Translation of The Torah* (Philadelphia: Jewish Publication Society of America, 1969), p. 170.

9. Cf. further, 81:5 ff.; 102:18 ff.; 106:7 ff.; 114; 118:13–16.

10. Cf. A Weiser, *The Psalms* (Philadelphia: Westminster Press, 1962), p. 792 f.

11. "It is not law and order itself, but the living God who created the universe and established its law and order, that stands supreme in biblical thought. . . . Before the Torah, the covenant was. In contrast to our civilization, the Hebrews lived in a world of the covenant rather than in a world of contracts. The idea of contract was unknown to them. The God of Israel 'cares as little for contract and the cash-nexus as He cares for mere slavish obedience and obsequiousness. His chosen sphere is that of covenant' (quoted from W. F. Lofthouse, 'Ḥen and Ḥesed in the Old Testament, ZAW, 51 [1933]: 29 ff). His relationship to his partner is one of benevolence and affection. The indispensable and living instrument holding the community of God and Israel together is the law." A. J. Heschel, The Prophets (New York: Harper & Row, 1962), p. 230. Cf. Robert Gordis, A Faith for Moderns (New York: Bloch, 1960), p. 153, and D. J. McCarthy, Old Testament Covenant: A Survey of Current Opinions (Oxford: Basil Blackwell, 1972), chap. 6.

12. Cf. Lev. 26:13; Deut. 27:9; 29:12: Jer. 7:23; 11:4; 13:11; 24:7; 30:22; 31:33; 32:38; Ezek. 11:20; 14:11; 34:24; 36:28; 37:23, 27; Zech. 8:8.

13. See H. Wheeler Robinson, Inspiration and Revelation in the Old Testament (Oxford: The Clarendon Press, 1964), p. 154. He regards this as the classic OT passage on "the grace of God in election."

14. Old Testament Essays on Old Testament History and Religion, trans. by R. A. Wilson (New York: Doubleday, 1968), p. 157.

15. Law and Covenant in Israel and the Ancient Near East (Pittsburgh: The Biblical Colloquium, 1955). Reprint from The Biblical Archaeologist, vol. 17, no. 2 (May 1954): 26–46 and no. 3 (Sept. 1954): 49–76.

16. The Covenant Formulary in Old Testament, Jewish and Early Christian Writings, trans. David E. Green (Philadelphia: Fortress Press, 1971).

17. The Interpreter's Bible, vol. 1 (New York-Nashville: Abingdon-Cokesbury Press, 1952), 980. W. Eichrodt speaks of the Passover as "an effective proclamation of the redeeming grace of God" in Theology of the Old Testament, vol. 1 (Philadelphia: Westminster Press, 1961), 129. See further his article on "Covenant and Law" Interpretation, 20 (1966): 302–321. W. Zimmerli says, "Der Bund aber ist reine Gnadenveranstaltung Gottes" in Th. Literaturzeitung, 85 (1960), col. 486, in commenting on M. Noth's, The Laws in the Pentateuch etc. (London: Oliver & Boyd, 1966), pp. 1–107.

18. The Old Testament: Its Formation and Development, trans. Dorothea M. Barton (New York: Association Press, 1961), p. 51, note. Cf. Herbert C. Alleman, "Obedience to the Unenforceable" in Religion in Life, 13 (1943–44): 107–113.

19. See G. A. F. Knight, op. cit. (see Introd., note 3), p. 27.

20. Cf. now H. W. Wolff, "The Day of Rest in the Old Testament" in Lexington Theological Quarterly, 7 (1972): 65–76. He calls attention especially to the Deuteronomic formulation (Deut. 5:15): "You shall remember that you were a slave in the land of Egypt, and Yahweh your God brought you out with a mighty hand and an outstretched arm; therefore Yahweh your God commanded you to keep the sabbath day." "Here the reason for observing the day of rest is that affirmation which was absolutely fundamental for Israel, namely, that Yahweh had liberated Israel from Egypt. On every sabbath Israel is to remember that her

God is a liberator who had put an end to all slave holding and who is a match for all who wield power within and without Israel, for all who might still seek to afflict his people (p. 67). . . . "The fundamental significance of the seventh day is therefore this: rest from our work is to remind us of the freedom we have already been given. . . . The sabbath commandment shows in an especially instructive way that the basic commandments are a great gift given to Israel to help and benefit her. Far from being demands, the Commandments are exactly the opposite: they free Israel from demands" (p. 68).

21. See G. von Rad, *The Problem of the Hexateuch and Other Essays*, trans. E. W. Trueman Dicken (New York: McGraw-Hill, 1966), pp. 3–8.

II
Grace and Torah
in the Early Prophets

From the days of Julius Wellhausen there has been serious discussion on the place of the prophets in the religious economy of Israel. Wellhausen believed that the prophets were essentially the creators of the religion of Israel. He wrote, "He (i.e., Moses) was the founder of the nation out of which the Torah and prophecy came as later growths." "Thus, although the prophets were far from originating a new conception of God, they nonetheless were the founders of what has been called 'ethical monotheism.' But with them this ethical monotheism was no product of the 'self-evolution of dogma,' but a progressive step which had been called forth simply by the course of events."[1] Later he said, "The prophets do not speak out of the law but out of the spirit; Yahweh speaks through them, not Moses. Their torah is worth just as much as that of Moses and issues from the same perennial source."[2] Most scholars today believe the oppostie is true, i.e., that the prophets stood on the shoulders of Moses;[3] they were thus reformers and not creators of the religion of Israel.

A. COVENANTAL TERMINOLOGY IN THE PROPHETS

One of the arguments employed to refute the prophetic dependence on the torah of Moses is the assertion that it is not possible to speak of a "definitive formulation of the idea of the covenant in the religious thought of Israel before the sixth century B.C."[4] A fair evaluation of the situation would require the assessment of each passage in the prophets as to its genuineness for which there is neither time nor space here. The statistics to follow are, therefore, rather general but revealing. The Hebrew term for covenant is b^erith which occurs a total of 285 times in the Old Testament, only seventy-three of which appear in the

23

prophetic books including Daniel. The general rendering by LXX is *diathēkē* which is found 270 times; *sunthēkē* is used only once to render *bᵉrith* (2 Kings, 17:15)—it is used more often by Aquila and Symmachus. Interestingly enough *diathēkē* occurs only thirty-three times in the New Testament, seven of which are in quotations from the LXX. It appears nine times in the Pauline writings, seventeen times in Hebrews, four times in the Synoptics, twice in Acts, and once in Revelation. Another word associated with covenant is *ḥesed,* found 247 times in the Old Testament, only twenty-nine times in the prophets including Daniel. *'ᵉmeth* appears 127 times in the Old Testament, forty of which are in the prophets and Daniel. *'ᵉmūnāh* related to it, occurs forty-nine times in the Old Testament, ten of which are in the prophets. Altogether, the four terms noted appear a total of 708 times in the Old Testament; in the prophets and Daniel 152 times or about 1/5 as many times.

Bible study by way of such statistics is quite unsatisfactory, often deceptive, but it does show that either the prophets themselves or the editors of their books were at least not ignorant of covenantal terminology. While it cannot be argued that the use of covenant expressions is profuse, it cannot at the same time be said that they are ignored in the prophets. The covenant only *appears* to be peripheral in prophetic theology. Lately there has been some effort to water down the significance of knowledge of the Mosaic covenant in prophetic literature. This attempt is without justification in the opinion of the writer. Nevertheless the problem as to why the prophets fail to use the actual word "covenant" does require some thought and attention. One reason for the prophets' general avoidance of the term has been suggested by Mendenhall.[5] The historical situation had changed markedly since Mosaic times, especially after the fall of Shiloh. In place of the old tribal confederation there developed a monarchy in which the basis of Yahweh's relationship with Israel shifted from the Mosaic covenant with its emphasis on Yahweh and the community to that of Yahweh and David. In other words the pattern of relationship followed was that of the Abrahamic covenant. The promises made to David with respect to the maintenance of his throne (2 Sam. 23:5) was similar to that made to Abraham and to Noah, "The covenant with Abraham was the 'prophecy' and that with David the 'fulfilment.' "[6] As Mendenhall goes on to show, this was followed in the south, though not in the north. There was no single dynastic establishment in the north, at least until the time of Omri. The prophets do not refer often to covenant because of the altered situation; the establishment pledged the continuance of the monarchy even though it violated the fundamental principles of Yahwism and so was under divine judgment. Moreover the prophetic insistence that Yahweh had determined to destroy the nation would, in effect, be accusing Yahweh of reneging on his covenant.

The prophets were certainly aware of the basic tenets of the Mosaic covenant inasmuch as they charged the nation rather than Yahweh with its violation. Mendenhall[7] notes five points that demonstrate such knowledge. First there was the "'I-You" form of address. Second, they called attention to Yahweh's benevolent acts antecedent to the peoples' disobedience or ingratitude which placed them under the curse. Third, they denounced sacrifice as a surrogate for ethical actions which they regarded as the true response to Yahweh's goodness as the Ten Words prescribed and as was the situation in the time of the confederation maintained only by religious sanctions. Fourth, they maintained a stance vis-à-vis all Israel and disclaimed the artificial division brought on by political events. In so doing they harked back to the early days of the confederation. Fifth, the prophets associated history with moral demands and so continued the Mosaic tradition.

It must not be overlooked that the prophets were critics of the king who, according to southern tradition, was the occupant of the throne of David. As observed above, the throne was covenanted to the Davidic dynasty.

> Your house and your kingdom shall be confirmed
>   before me forever;
> For all time your throne shall be established (2 Sam. 7:16).

The monarchy, therefore, assumed the place of Israel in the Mosaic covenant and Yahweh's covenant was with it rather than with the community. The covenant with David had replaced the covenant with "my people"; and, since the prophets inveighed against the king, threatening him and his kingdom with extinction, they found themselves in a dilemma. They could hardly maintain the validity of an eternal covenant with David and at the same time bring the monarchy under divine judgment. Hence, as Mendenhall says, they simply ignored it for the most part. But that does not mean that they were unfamiliar with the Mosaic covenant or that their failure to mention it specifically as a basis for their invectives indicates its non-existence. It is indeed hard to see how the Deuteronomist, whose theology is so firmly rooted in the Mosaic tradition, could have introduced an entirely new conception, as some assert, to counter the Davidic covenant without some historic precedent.[8]

B. COVENANT TERMINOLOGY IN THE EARLY PROPHETS

The only certain passage in which *berith* is used is Hos. 8:1:

> To your mouth [put] the trumpet;
> Like an eagle over the house of Yahweh![9]
> Because they have transgressed my covenant,
> And rebelled against my torah.

The parallelism between "my covenant" and "my torah" reflects the old conception current at least in the north. The reference to the house of Yahweh here is to the land in which Israel dwells and not to the sanctuary. The prophet thus announces the imminent threat to the land, pronounces the curse against the people who have broken Yahweh's covenant and rejected his torah. The passage is reminiscent of the complaint of Elijah to Yahweh —"They have abandoned your covenant" (I Kings 19:10, 14)— and the subsequent curse pronounced upon Ahab and his house (I Kings 21:21–24).

An even more striking phenomenon is the reference of the eighth century prophets to the exodus experience. Speaking of the Assyrian threat, Isaiah says: "O my people, who dwell in Zion, be not afraid of the Assyrians when they smite with the rod and lift up their staff against you as the Egyptians did. . . . And the Lord of hosts will wield against them a scourge, as when he smote Midian at the rock of Oreb; and his rod will be over the sea, and he will lift it as he did in Egypt" (10:24, 26). In 11:16 he refers to "Israel when they came up from the land of Egypt." The same reference occurs in Hosea (2:15; 12:14). Another very significant declaration of Hosea is, "I am Yahweh your God, from the land of Egypt" (12:9; 13:4). But perhaps his most trenchant observation is, "When Israel was a child, I loved him, and out of Egypt I called my son" (11:1). Several times he speaks of Israel having to return to Egypt to relearn the saving concern of Yahweh for his people and their dependence on him alone as their God and deliverer (8:13; 9:3; 11:5). Amos too speaks of Yahweh's deliverance of Israel out of Egypt (2:10; 3:1; 9:7). In 4:10 he says "I sent among you a pestilence after the manner of Egypt." Micah echoes the same sentiment with reference to Israel's being brought out of Egypt by Yahweh (6:4; 7:15).

W. Eichrodt[10] and F. Charles Fensham[11] have independently called attention to the father-son or family relationship conceptions and vocabulary in treaty structures of the ancient Near East. It is well-known that the term father applied to God is rare in the Old Testament, probably because of its connection with the fertility cult of Baal. But Israel as Yahweh's son(s) occurs more often. E.g., Moses was instructed to say to the Pharaoh, "Israel is my firstborn son . . . let my son go that he may serve me" (Exod. 4:22, 23 [J and Nomadic]). That pattern is found also in the prophets. Only a few can be cited here. Isaiah proclaims: "Sons have I reared and brought up, but they have rebelled against me" (1:2) and "sons who deal corruptly" (1:4). Carrying through the theme of wayward Israel, he says: "For they are a rebellious people, lying sons, sons who will not listen to the instruction of Yahweh" (30.9). Hosea calls Israel "sons of the living God" (1:10). The classic passage, however, is 11:1 ff.:

> When Israel was a child, I loved him,
> And out of Egypt I called my son.
> The more I called them,
> The farther they went from me;
> They kept sacrificing to Baal,
> And burning incense to idols.
> Yet, I taught Ephraim to walk,
> I took them up in my arms,
> But they did not know that I healed them.
> I led them with human cords,
> With bands of love,
> And I was to them
> Like one who lifts the suckling to the cheeks,
> And I bent down to them and fed them.

Surely here is not only a conception of deliverance from Egypt but one of a tender relationship involved in the gift of the torah which was meant to instruct Yahweh's sons in the way of peace and blessing. Such terms as bride and bridegroom (Hosea) and

27

the beloved (Isa, 5:1 ff.) also occur. The prophets, of course, lament Israel's apostasy which marked the breakdown of the most intimate relationship that should have obtained in the light of Yahweh's upbringing and care for his sons.

Closely related to this is the concept of Yahweh's people. According to Exod 6:7 (P) Yahweh says to Moses, "I will take you for my people and I will be your God." While the expression may be late (cf. its use in Jeremiah), the concept is not. Obviously when Yahweh is the speaker, the latter part of the formula would be superfluous. Hence the phrase "my people" in Exod. 3:7, 10; 5:1; 7:4, 16; 8:1, 20–23; 9:1. Already by Yahweh's election and determination, he had adopted them as his people so that the declaration "my people" is already a covenant term. Only by his grace could they become and be his people. Now the same expression appears in Isaiah (1:3; 2:12, 15; 5:13; 10:2, 24), Hosea (1:9, 10; 2:23; 4:6, 8, 12; 6:11; 11:7), Amos (7:15; 8:2; 9:10), and Micah (1:9; 2:4, 8, 9; 3:3, 5; 6:3, 5) which indicates that these prophets knew and used this peculiar covenant term in the promulgation of their messages.

Several other words that appear to have been associated with the covenant may be mentioned here. In the great victory hymn in Exod. 15:13 we read

> You have led with your *ḥesed,*
> The people whom you have redeemed;
> You have led them by your strength,
> To your holy abode.

The expanded section of the commandment against making graven images asserts God's *"ḥesed* to thousands of those who love me and keep my commandments" (Exod. 20:6). The J document speaks of Yahweh's "abounding in *ḥesed* and *'emeth,* keeping *ḥesed* for thousands, forgiving iniquity and transgression and sin, but who will by no means clear the guilty . . ." (34:6, 7). Both *ḥesed*[12] and *'emeth* are associated with Yahweh's loyalty and devotion to the covenant fellowship with his people. Under the figure of the marriage bond, Yahweh says through Hosea: "I will betroth you to me forever; I will betroth you to me in righteousness and in justice, in *ḥesed* and in compassion. I will betroth you to me in *'emeth*" (2:19–20a). Yahweh's complaint is that "there is no *'emeth* or *ḥesed* . . . in the land" (4:1). What are Yahweh's de-

28

mands—"delight in *ḥesed* (covenant loyalty) and not sacrifice, the knowledge of God rather than burnt offerings" (6:6). Among other qualities, Micah says Yahweh requires *ḥesed* of his people (6:8) any delights in *ḥesed* (7:18). Of Yahweh he declares, "You will show *'emeth* to Jacob and *ḥesed* to Abraham as you have sworn to our fathers from of old" (7:20). The prophetic passages mirror the same character exhibited in the covenant relationship. If anything they are more definite in meaning than the covenant appellative itself.

A few years ago Herbert B. Huffman[13] published an article in which he pointed out the covenantal significance of the Hebrew word *yāda'* (to know), by calling attention to its technical use in Hittite and Akkadian treaties, and in the Bible. Employed in that sense it signifies a reciprocal recognition on the part of the suzerain and the vassal. A number of passages have been noted by Huffman that bear this meaning but we must confine ourselves to the early writing prophets.

> "My people go into exile for lack of knowledge" (Isa. 5:13).

> "You only have I known[14]
> Of all the families of the earth;
> Therefore I will punish you
> For all your iniquities" (Amos 3:2).

The former refers to the failure of Israel to observe and live by the covenant, i.e., her recognition of the grace and power of Yahweh who has redeemed her and given her the torah for her guidance; therefore she has broken the covenant .The Amos piece is even more positive. There *yāda'* has the meaning of choose and clearly points to something more than acquaintance. "You alone have I chosen (by entering into covenant with you)" and since the covenant had been violated Yahweh exercises his suzerain obligations. Or take the statement of Hosea:

> I am Yahweh your God
> From the land of Egypt.
> And gods except me you will not know;
> There is no savior beside me.
> I knew you in the wilderness,
> In a land of drought (Hos. 13:4,5)

which unmistakably refers to the Egyptian desert experience of Israel. Deliverance from Egypt is mentioned together with the caution to avoid entering into any similar relationship with other gods. But the prophet also stresses the continuance of Yahweh's saving acts in the desert whereby he fulfilled his covenant obligations to his chosen people. Furthermore, when he castigates Israel because he sees "no knowledge of God in the land" (4:1) and declares "my people are destroyed for lack of knowledge" (4:6), he laments the absence of covenant response on the part of the people. Observe also the direct connection between "covenant" and "know" in 8:1–3:

> . . . they have broken my covenant,
> And transgressed my torah.
> [yet] to me they cry,
> 'My God, we, Israel know you.
> Israel has spurned good;
> An enemy will pursue him.

The exclamation "'My God, we, Israel know you" here does not mean simply "we are informed about you" but rather "we recognize you as Lord, as sovereign." Yet the actions and deeds of the nation indicate otherwise, thus necessitating the pronouncement of the curse associated with the covenant obligations of the sovereign. On the other hand, recollection of the blessings of Yahweh, upholding his sovereign obligations in the past, augur well for the present and future, according to Micah.

> O my people, remember what Balak, king of Moab, contrived,
> And how Balaam, the son of Beor, responded to him,
> And [what happened] from Shittim to Gilgal,
> That you may know the saving acts of Yahweh (6:5).

Knowledge of the saving acts of Yahweh here means recognition of his covenant deeds that continued to be manifest after the events at Sinai. He would continue his blessings to his people if they recognized him as Lord and remained subject to him.

One of the features of the covenant was the announcement of blessings and curses (Deut. 28) attendant upon its observance or its violation. This theme is also present in the prophets. The song of the vineyard in Isaiah (5:1 ff.) tells of the continued blessings of Yahweh.

> My beloved had a vineyard
> On a fertile hill;
> He trenched it and cleared it of stones,
> And planted it with choice vines;

> He built a watchtower in the midst of it,
> And hewed out a wine vat in it;
> And he looked for it to yield grapes
> But it yielded wild grapes.

Amos surveying the then and now says of Yahweh:

> Yet I destroyed the Amorite before them,
> Whose height was like that of the cedars,
> And who was as strong as the oaks;
> I destroyed his fruit above,
> And his roots beneath.
> Moreover, I brought you up out of the land of Egypt,
> And led you forty years in the wilderness,
> To possess the land of the Amorite.
> And I raised up some of your sons for prophets,
> And some of your young men for Nazirites.
> Is it not just so, O people of Israel? (2:9–11)

Hosea is equally aware of Yahweh's blessings, particularly as they pertain to daily life and sustenance:

> . . . it was I who gave her
> the grain, the wine, and the oil,
> and who lavished upon her silver
> and gold which they used for Baal (2:8).

The divine pathos of which he writes (11:1 ff.) has already been quoted to illustrate the prophet's understanding of deliverance from slavery and bondage together with Israel's upbringing in the desert and, subsequently, Micah, giving voice to Yahweh's lament over wayward Israel, bursts out

> O my people, what have I done to you?
> In what have I wearied you? Tell me!
> For I brought you up from the land of Egypt,
> And redeemed you from the house of slaves
> And sent before you Moses,
> Aaron and Miriam (6:3–4).

Because of the nation's continual spurning of these great blessings, her failure on every count to appreciate the manifold gifts of her sovereign Lord, and her persistent recalcitrance, Yahweh had no alternative but to invoke the covenant provision of curses. That is why the prophetic literature is so full of threats and judgment. It was doubtless the hope of the prophets to jolt the people out of their lethargy and indifference to a rededication to and appreciation of their covenant obligations to their savior, redeemer, and sustainer. But the more Yahweh called to them the more they went from him (Hos. 11:2a), so that he was constrained to invoke the curses of the covenant. That is the import e.g., of the woes pronounced by Isaiah:

> Woe to those who join house to house,
> Who add field to field! (5:8a)

> Woe to those who rise early in the morning,
> That they may run after strong drink,
> Who tarry late in the evening
> Till wine inflames them! (5:11)

> Woe to those who draw iniquity with cords of falsehood,
> Who draw sin as with cart ropes! (5:18)

> Woe to those who call evil good and good evil,
> Who put darkness for light and light for darkness,
> Who put bitter for sweet and sweet for bitter! (5:20)

> Woe to those who are wise in their own eyes,
> And shrewd in their own sight! (5:21)

> Woe to those who are heroes at drinking wine,
> And valiant in mixing strong drink,
> Who acquit the guilty for a bribe,
> And deprive the innocent of their right! (5:22)

Listen to the devastating judgment voiced by Amos against the women of Samaria:

> Hear this word, you cows of Bashan,
> Who are in the mountain of Samaria,
> Who oppress the poor and crush the needy,
> Who say to their husbands,
> 'Bring that we may drink!'
> The Lord God has sworn by his holiness
> That, behold, days are coming upon you,
> When they shall take you away with hooks,
> Even the last of you with fishhooks.
> And you shall go out through the breaches,
> Every one straight in front of her,
> And you will be thrown out into Harman (exile land?) (4:1–3)

Then he proceeds to sing a dirge over the house of Israel:

> Fallen, no more to rise,
> Is the virgin Israel;
> Forsaken on her land,
> With no one to raise her up (5:2).

Even the more gentle Hosea says:

> Therefore I am like a moth to Ephraim,
> And like blight to the house of Judah (5:12).

> For I will be like a lion to Ephraim,
> Like a young lion to the house of Judah.
> I will, even I, rend asunder and depart,
> I will carry off and there will be no one to rescue (5:14).

Because of Israel's contumacy, Micah speaking in the name of Yahweh says:

> Therefore I will make Samaria a tell in a field,
> A place for planting vineyards;
> And I will pour down her stones into the valley,
> And lay bare her foundations (1:6).

> Make yourselves bald and cut off your hair,
> For the children of your delight;
> Make yourselves as bald as the eagle,
> For they shall go into exile from you (1:16).

C. THE TORAH AND THE PROPHETS

Perhaps the most crucial contact of the prophets with the covenant implications has to do with the Torah. We must remember that torah does not mean law in our sense of the term. There is some disagreement about the etymology of the word[15] but whatever view one takes of that is immaterial for our purpose. It is clear that its meaning in the biblical context of the covenant is teaching, guidance, instruction. The torah was not given as an instrument of salvation for Israel; it was rather the gracious act of Yahweh revealing to his delivered people his expectations for them as his people. It was thus the revelation of his will in whose observance Israel could maintain her salvation and express her gratitude for his saving and sustaining acts.

1. Violations of the Basic Covenant Principles

It has been said that the Decalogue (the Ten Words, never called commandments) was conceived along broad lines that were capable of application in every age. That is essentially so but there is some evidence that the prophets assumed the authority of the Decalogue,[16] sometimes referred to it directly. A few instances must suffice in support of that statement. It is pretty generally

agreed that the prophets insisted on at least a practical monotheism. As early as Elijah, there is attestation to the fact that they
took for granted the nonexistence of other deities. Perhaps Isaiah
had in mind the first word of the Decalogue when he complained
that Judah and Israel had "forsaken Yahweh and spurned the
Holy One of Israel" (1:4). The second word with its warning
against images is surely in the purview of Hosea when he says
"A maker of images is Ephraim" (4:17); "of their silver and the
gold they made idols for themselves" (8:4);

> And now they sin more and more,
> In that they make for themselves molten images,
> All of them the work of craftsmen.
> "Sacrifice to these," they cry,
> Men kissing calves. (13:2).

Every prophet from Elijah to the exile echoes the same sentiment
because experience had demonstrated how relevant the second
word was in the proscribing of image making; how tempting and
easy it was to define the divine so as to make it conform to the
human conceptual pattern! (cf. Isa. 2:8). Not much is said by the
prophets about the misuse of Yahweh's name, though it is implied
in every denunciation of the application of it to that which Yahweh did not command. There are frequent hints of the transgression of the third word in connection with the multiplication of
altars and high places where aberrations occurred and where Baal
was worshipped under the guise of Yahweh's name, or where Yahweh was worshipped with Baalistic trappings. The sabbath word
does not seem to have been stressed by the early prophets, though
there is a veiled reminder of its sanctity in Amos 8:5.[17]
Micah complains bitterly that

> . . . the son treats the father with contempt,
> the daughter rises up against her mother,
> the daughter-in-law against her mother-in-law;
> a man's enemies are the men of his own house (7:6).

The word about murder is reflected in all the prophets though it
is not specifically quoted; they take it for granted. Hosea, lament-
ing the lack of knowledge (covenant recognition), says there is

> swearing and lying,   murdering and stealing,
> commission of adultery—   they are on the increase
> so that blood touches blood (4:2).

34

Isaiah affirms "your hands are full of blood" (1:15) and Yahweh "looked for justice, but behold bloodshed" (5:7). One of the most heinous practices, from the prophetic point of view, was adultery which threatened the family and hence the stability of the nation. The seventh word laid down the principle that murder could not be condoned in a covenant society. Hosea's complaint has already been noted; in another outburst he cries

> They are all adulterers;
> They are like a heated oven (7:4a).

Later prophets also speak out against it (Jer. 7:9; 23:14; Ezek. 23:37, 43 ff.; Mal. 3:5). The eighth word, against stealing, was emphasized also by Hosea (4:2; 7:1). He deplores false dealing too (7:1) and affirms that "their heart is false" (10:2). Words nine and ten go together and may be the most widely infringed upon principle in the Decalogue. One could perhaps take the last three words together, the last two depicting methods by which the first of the three may be contrived. Recall St. Paul's observation: "I should not have known what it is to covet if the law had not said, 'You shall not covet.' But sin, finding opportunity in the commandment, wrought in me all kinds of covetousness" (Rom. 7:7b–8a). How does one actually steal? He may of course do it overtly. But he may also deprive his neighbor of his rights by bearing false witness in court against him. Or he may deprive his neighbor of his land and property by illicit appropriation as J. Hermann long ago insisted.[18] The best illustration of this point is Micah 2:1–2:

> Woe to those who plot wickedness
> And perpetrate evil upon their beds!
> When the morning dawns, they do it,
> Because it is in the power of their hands.
> They covet fields and take them;
> And houses, and seize them;
> They oppress a man and his house,
> A man and his inheritance.

Here coveting and seizure are in parallelism. How they did it may be seen from the following passages. They showed partiality; "Their partiality testifies against them" (Isa. 3:9a); they were guilty of bribery:

> Your princes are rebels,
> And companions of thieves.

Every one loves a bribe
And pursues after gifts.
They do not defend the fatherless,
And the widow's cause does not move them" (Isa. 1:23).

They arranged mortgages in such a way that they could foreclose within the law as Isaiah laments:

Woe to those who join house to house,
Who add field to field,
Until there is no room left,
And you are made to dwell alone
In the midst of the land (5:8).

They conspired against the unfortunate and helpless yeoman by

. . . acquitting the guilty for a bribe,
And depriving the innocent of his right (Isa. 5:23).

Woe to those who decree unrighteous decrees,
And the recorders who record false records (*'ml*),
To deprive the needy of justice,
And rob the poor of my people of their rights,
So that widows become their booty,
And that they may plunder the fatherless! (Isa. 10:1).

They are motivated by treachery (Hos. 7:3, 16b) so that

Ephraim surrounds me with lies,
And the house of Israel with deceit (Hos. 11:12).

2. *The Moral Toroth*

Broader aspects of the prophet-torah relationship may be judged by a brief account of their views on social justice. Wellhausen attributed the moral law to the prophets and not to Moses. But he says, "the simple ideas of the prophets did not provide a medium for the establishment of a community; they themselves required a structure so as not to be lost to the world. The legal cultus provided that structure. Out of originally pagan material a panzer was forged for the monotheism of morals."[19] To some extent that is a correct observation, for it is altogether likely that instruction in the torah was transmitted within the covenant community. However, it was the *torah of Moses* that was thus handed down; the prophets interpreted, applied, insisted upon its validity, and called down Yahweh's judgment upon those who neglected it.

The covenant, on its human side, was one of brotherhood. Yahweh's people were his adopted sons, hence brothers, which fact necessitated the recognition of social rights and duties, as well as privileges and immunities. One cannot read the prophets without one eye on the torah, especially the dicta of the book of the covenant which was early regarded as the fundamental law of Israel.[20] While many of the precedents are obviously casuistic in nature, they fall in line with the gracious will of Yahweh for his people. The so-called *mishpāṭim* consist of special cases that were to be handled with *mishpāṭ,* i.e., with justice, having due regard for one's claims for that which is right. The term occurs nineteen times in Isaiah 1, four each in Amos and Hosea, and five in Micah,[21] which is an index of its importance in the thinking of these prophets. Isaiah tells his hearers to "seek *mishpāṭ*" (1:17), that "Yahweh of hosts is exalted through *mishpāṭ*" (5:16), and that the messiah is to be characterized by *mishpāṭ* (9:7). Yahweh is a God of *mishpāṭ* (30:18). Hosea predicts that Yahweh's *mishpāṭim* "shall go forth like light" (6:5) and that *mishpāṭ* will blossom forth like weeds in the furrows of the field (10:4c). Amos complains, "you turn *mishpāṭ* to gall" (5:7) and calls upon his people to "establish *mishpāṭ* in the gate" (5:15). In a well-known passage he exhorts:

> But let *mishpāṭ* roll down like waters,
> And righteousness like an ever flowing stream (5:24).

Micah accuses the magnates of Israel of abhorring *mishpāṭ* and distorting everything that is right (3:9). It was in their place "to know *mishpāṭ*" (3:1). His most familiar dictum is

> Yet what does Yahweh require of you,
> But to do *mishpāṭ*, and to love *ḥesed,*
> And to walk humbly with your God? (6:8).

The covenant code has a great deal to say about human indenture (Exod. 21:2), the treatment of the stranger (Exod. 22:21; 23:9), lending money to one's covenant fellow (Exod: 22:21), even the humane treatment of animals (Exod. 23:5). The most incisive interdiction reads: "You must not pervert *mishpāṭ* due to the poor in his case" (Exod. 23:6). Elijah has been called the champion of the common man and Elisha was found pleading the cause of those who were in trouble or whose rights were in jeopardy. This was the tradition carried on by the writing prophets of the eighth century. Isaiah castigated transgressors in no uncertain terms.

> Your princes are rebellious,
> And fellow-travelers with thieves.
> All of them love a bribe,
> And run after donations.
> They do not support the (cause of the) orphan,
> Nor does the case of the widow ever reach them (Isa. 1:23).

Against the elders of the people he hurls the indictment:

> You have ravaged the vineyard—
> Goods robbed from the poor are in your houses.
> What do you mean by beating down my people,
> And grinding the faces of the poor? (Isa. 3:14b).

Amos' accusation is even more devastating: the judgment of Yahweh will not turn aside.

> Because they sell the innocent for a price,
> The needy for a pair of sandals.
> They grind the heads of the defenseless into the ground,
> And push the humble out of the way (2:6b–7a).

> You oppress the righteous, take hush money,
> And throw the poor out of court (5:12).

> [They] make the measure small and the price high,
> And falsify the scales,
> Buy the poor for a price,
> And the needy for a pair of sandals,
> And sell the offal of the wheat (8:5–6).

Micah charges:

> They devour the flesh of my people,
> They strip off their skin from upon them,
> Break in pieces their bones,
> And shred them like meat in the pot,
> Like flesh in a cauldron (3:3).

D. THE GOD OF THE PROPHETS

The God of the prophets was the God of Moses, the covenant God, who delivered his people from slavery and bondage and graciously offered them principles by which they might remain his people, enjoy his blessings, avoid the curses, and perform his

service in the land promised to the fathers as an eternal possession. As we have seen, there is a multitude of references to these
matters in the early prophetic literature, more in that of the later
prophets and in the Deuteronomic literature which have not
come into consideration for obvious reasons.

The holy God of Exod. 3:5 and the holy nation concept of
Exod. 19:6 run through the prophets. The phrase the Holy One
of Israel occurs in ten passages of Isaiah (1:4; 5:19, 24; 10:17;
29:19; 30:11b, 15; 31:1; 37:23; cf. also 5:16; 6:3).[22] This designation refers to all Israel as Yahweh's people, not just to Judah. As
Eichrodt points out, more is involved here than cultic holiness.
The Holy One of Israel "becomes for Isaiah in the hour of his
call an expression of the moral power above the world. As such,
it indeed annihilates the sinner but draws the penitent into its
sphere through its absolution in order to make him the herald of
its coming rule over the world."[23] Isaiah's vision of the Holy One
of Israel in the temple, present in the midst of Israel, is reminiscent of his presence among his people in the whole of the exodus
experience. He was not a far away God but one near at hand, and
as interested and concerned with Israel now as then.[24] If one can
speak of Yahweh's immanence, he can at the same time take
cognizance of the fact that the prophets were in place of Moses
and the torah. In other words Yahweh had not abandoned Israel
as his sending of the prophets demonstrated. They were certainly
critics of king, priests, and nation but they censored them for their
contumacious ingratitude exhibited by injustice, idolatry, licentiousness, immorality, and inconsiderateness of the poor and
oppressed. They regarded disobedience not simply as violation
of the law but as ingratitude for Yahweh's beneficent acts from
Egypt to the present day. He promised to be with them always
and he was. He had not broken his word, his covenant, but the
people had broken theirs.

Down to the very end of the Old Testament, the great religious
leaders retained their faith in Yahweh's presence with his people.
Even in the exile, in distant Babylon, he did not abandon them.
Ezekiel's new city was to be called *Yahweh šāmmāh* (48:35). The
full realization of Yahweh's abiding grace is proclaimed in Jesus
Christ, our savior, whose act of salvation too is accompanied by a
torah—the sermon on the mount. This also reveals his grace. Our
response in gratitude thereto confers blessings upon us.

It is highly significant that the prophets speak of a return to Egypt to relive the experience of deliverance from bondage and the re-establishment of the covenantal relationship between Yahweh and his people.[25]

> But Ephraim shall return to Egypt,
> And in Assyria they shall eat unclean food. Hos. 9:3b.

> Therefore, thus will I do to you, O Israel.
> Because I shall do this to you,
> Prepare to meet your God, O Israel. (Probably a secondary passage from Amos. 4:12).

> On that day the Lord will whistle for the fly
> (That is beyond the streams of Egypt),
> And the bee (that is in the land of Assyria). Isa. 7:18—parentheses indicate additions.

NOTES

1. J. Wellhausen, *Sketch of the History of Israel and Judah* (London and Edinburgh: A. & C. Black, 3d ed. 1891), pp. 19, 88.

2. Quoted by W. Zimmerli, "Das Gesetz im Alten Testament" in *Th. LZ,* 85 (1960), col. 483, n. 3. Cf. Wellhausen, *Prolegomena to the History of Israel* (Edinburgh: A. & C. Black, 1885), pp. 399 ff.—"It is a vain imagination to suppose that the prophets expounded and applied the law."

3. See, e.g., G. E. Wright, *IB*, 1 (New York-Nashville, Abingdon-Cokesbury Press, 1952): 355a; J. Muilenberg, *ibid.,* p. 300; H. Wheeler Robinson, *Inspiration and Revelation in the Old Testament* (Oxford: The Clarendon Press, 1946), p. 154; John Bright, *A History of Israel* (Philadelphia: Westminster Press, 1960), p. 132 f.). There is now some questioning of this covenant conception. Cf. C. F. Whitley, "Covenant and Commandment" in *JNES*, 22 (1963): 37–48; G. Fohrer, "Altes Testament—'Amphiktyonie' und 'Bund'?," *Theologische Literaturzeitung* 91 (1966), cols 801–816, 893–904. Fohrer says ". . . a true 'covenant' theology had its inception with Deuteronomy, and the *berith* conception is only one of several conceptual terms for the relationship between Yahweh and Israel; during the nomadic period the idea of the community preponderated, in later times that of the dominion of God" (col. 901). See also E. Kutsch, "Der Begriff Berith in vordeuteronomischer Zeit" in *Das Ferne und Nahe Wort* (Festschrift Leonhard Rost), ed. F. Maass (Berlin: Töpelmann, 1967), pp. 132–143; and R. E. Clements, *Prophecy and Covenant* (London: SCM Press, 1965); A. Jepsen, "Berith: Ein Beitrag zur Theologie der Exilszeit" in *Verbannung und Heimkehr* (W. Rudolph Festschrift), ed. A. Kuschke (Tübingen: J. C. B. Mohr [Paul Siebeck], 1961), pp. 161–179.

4. W. Eichrodt, "Prophet and Covenant: Observations on the Exegesis of Isaiah" in *Proclamation and Presence. Old Testament Essays in Honour of Gwynne Henton Davies*, ed. J. I. Durham and J. R. Porter (London: SCM Press, 1970), p. 167.

5. *Law and Covenant in Israel and the Ancient Near East* (Pittsburgh: The Biblical Colloquium, 1955), p. 46.

6. *Ibid.*, p. 46.

7. *Ibid.*, p. 46 f.

8. For further arguments on this point see W. Eichrodt, *op. cit.*, pp. 183–188.

9. The Targum paraphrases, "Behold, like an eagle, that soars, a king rises up with his host and approaches the house of Yahweh's sanctuary. . . ."

10. *Op. cit.*, pp. 172 ff.

11. "Father and Son as Terminology for Treaty and Covenant" in *Near Eastern Studies in Honor of William Foxwell Albright*, ed. Hans Goedicke (Baltimore: Johns Hopkins Press, 1971), pp. 121–135.

12. See N. H. Snaith, *The Distinctive Ideas of the Old Testament* (London: The Epworth Press, 1944), pp. 94–130.

13. "The Treaty Background of Hebrew *Yada'*" in *BASOR*, 181 (1966): 31–37.

14. Cf. Walter Harrelson, *Interpreting the Old Testament* (New York: Holt, Rinehart, and Winston, Inc., 1964), p. 346.

15. See W. F. Albright's discussion in *JBL*, 46 (1927): 182 ff., which he still held in 1957; *From the Stone Age to Christianity*, 2nd ed. (New York: Doubleday Anchor Books, 1957), p. 220, n. 30; p. 270, n. 96; also N. W. Porteous, "The Basis for the Ethical Teaching of the Prophets" in *Studies in Old Testament Prophecy* (T. H. Robinson Fetschrift), ed. H. H. Rowley (Edinburgh: T. & T. Clark, 1950), p. 148.

16. Cf. W. Eichrodt, *Theology of the Old Testament*, trans. J. A. Baker (Philadelphia: Westminster Press, vol. 1, 1961), p. 364. For the occurrence elsewhere in the Old Testament of the prohibitions of the Decalogue see A. Alt, *Old Testament History and Religion*, trans. R. A. Wilson (New York: Doubleday Anchor Books, 1968), pp. 151–158, esp. tables on p. 156 f.

17. "Hear this, you who trample upon the needy,
    And bring the poor of the land to an end,
    Saying, 'When will the new moon be over,
    That we may sell grain?
    And the sabbath,
    That we may offer wheat for sale.'"

18. "Das Zehnte Gebot" in *Sellin-Festschrift* (Leipzig: A Deichertsche Verlagbuchhandlung D. Werner Scholl, 1927), pp. 69–82, esp. pp. 71–75; cf. J. J. Stamm, *Der Dekalog im Lichte der neueren Forschung* (Bern: Verlag Paul Haupt, 1958), pp. 46–50.

19. Quoted by W. Zimmerli, *op cit.*, col. 484.

20. B. Baentsch, *Das Bundesbuch* (Halle: Niemeyer, 1892), p. 117— "Die Propheten Amos und Micah stehen ganz in der Sphäre des Bundesbuch."

21. Occurs 425 times in the Hebrew Bible.

22. These passages are discussed by W. Eichrodt in the article cited above, n. 4, pp. 169–172.

23. *Ibid.*, p. 170. Amos charges the people with the profanation of Yahweh's holy name (2:7); Yahweh swears by his holiness (4:2). Hosea too speaks of him as the Holy One (11:12). On Amos see Frank H. Seilhamer, "The Role of Covenant in the Mission and Message of Amos" in *A Light unto My Path: Old Testament Studies in Honor of Jacob M. Myers*, ed H. N. Bream, R. D. Heim, C. A. Moore (Philadelphia: Temple University Press, 1974), pp. 435–451.

24. Hosea has Yahweh declare that he is The Holy One in your midst (11:9).

25. W. Zimmerli, in connection with the prophets' pronouncement of judgment, notes that "It (the prophets' announcement of Yahweh's judgment) has to do with Yahweh's inevitable confrontation with Israel. Proclaimed here is not an event hidden from view in a struggle with the nations of the world but one that is consummated between Yahweh and his people. Certainly this occurrence is not an inner or secret one limited to religious thought or mental contemplation behind the affairs of international history, but, insofar as it is an occurrence in which Yahweh speaks to his people, it is nevertheless at the same time an altogether historical happening in the world of nations. But how much this historical happening is wholly one between Yahweh and his people wherein Yahweh's voice will not be drowned out by that of a terrestrial super power is reflected by the peculiar phenomenon that Amos does not name specifically a mighty power to bring about Israel's deportation and 'end.' Whoever the power responsible for deportation and 'end' may be it is decisive that Israel experience and recognize therein the encounter with her God." *Studies in the Religion of Ancient Israel* (Leiden: Brill, 1972), p. 53. For further observations on this type of thought in Israel see W. Zimmerli, *Die Weltlichkeit des Alten Testament* (Göttingen: Vandenhoeck & Ruprecht, 1971).

III

Grace and Torah in Deuteronomy and the Later Prophets

While the basic pattern reflected in the preceding chapters remains intact, there is a somewhat different emphasis in Deuteronomy and the later prophets, especially those before the exile. A strict documentary analysis is not called for here, though the several sections of Deuteronomy do bear careful consideration, e.g., chapters 1–11, 12–26, 28; 27; and the great poetic chapters, 32 and 33.

A. THE DEUTERONOMIC REFORMATION

The Deuteronomic reformation was not a spontaneous affair. It is hardly possible that there was no thought about Judah, her fortunes, and the covenant with Yahweh in the nearly half century preceding the accession of Josiah (640–609 B.C.). The reign of Hezekiah, especially in the later years, was beset with international problems,[1] whose complications were of far-reaching consequences as may be seen from Assyrian hegemony during the reign of Manasseh (687–642 B.C.) and Amon (642–640 B.C.). Although the conservative Yahwists went underground they did not remain inactive. (Cf. e.g., the name of Zephaniah = Yahweh has hidden.) The prophetic threats against Judah and Jerusalem reported by the writer of 2 Kings 21:11–15 sound much like those uttered by Amos against Israel (2:6–16). The early portion of the reign of Josiah coincided with the rapid decline of Assyrian power in the west largely because of the persistent troubles that beset Asshurbanipal in the east[2] and the resurgence of Egypt in the west.

The Chronicler reports that Josiah's reforming activity began in the eighth year of his kingship (2 Chron. 34:3–7)[3] while he was still under a regency characterized by some moderation. To judge from the prophecy of Zephaniah (ca. 630 B.C.), the Yahwists were beginning to surface. The climate for such activity was more propitious because of the hand taken in the succession by the *'ām hā'āreṣ* after the murder of Amon. As might be expected both Kings and Chronicles regard Josiah as a religious as well as a family descendant of David, the classical Yahwist king. Chronicles says that in his twelfth year (629/8 B.C.) Josiah "began to purge from Judah and Jerusalem the high places, the Asherahs, and the carved and molten images. He smashed the altars of Baal, cut to pieces the incense altars that were above them, broke up and pulverized the Asherahs and the carved and molten images, and strewed [the dust] before the graves of those who sacrificed to them. He burned the bones of their priests upon their altars and thus cleansed Judah and Jerusalem" (2 Chron. 34:3–5). The last great Assyrian king Asshurbanipal died in the fourteenth year of Josiah's reign (ca. 628/7 B.C.). Josiah made no overt move to renounce Judah's vassalage to Assyria at this time; he may even have regarded himself as a sort of caretaker of the territory of Israel after the demise of the Assyrian king and extended his purge to "the cities of Manasseh, Ephraim, and Simeon as far as Naphtali" (2 Chron. 34:6) under his self-appropriated authority. In any event, the reform movement began before the reformation itself took place.

It could well be that the initial reforming activity of Josiah was inspired by Zephaniah's unequivocal denunciation of Judah and proclamation of the day of Yahweh. He pronounces

> Woe to the defiant and defiled one, the oppressing city!
> She listened to no voice,
> She accepted no instruction.
> She did not trust Yahweh,
> To her God she did not draw near.
> Her princes within her are raging lions;
> Her judges have left no bones [for the morning].
> Her prophets are unreliable, perfidious men;
> Her priests have profaned what is holy;
> They have done violence to *tôrāh* (3:1–4).

While the covenant is not mentioned here, the implication is clear. The nation's leaders have renounced the torah, they have rejected discipline, and they have shown singular ingratitude for what Yahweh had done and will still do if they accept his instruction and draw near to him. Zephaniah's announcement of judgment must have been in the mind of Josiah when he evidenced such alarm on hearing the book of the torah read for the first time (2 Kings 22:11). Moreover, the prophet proclaimed, as oracle of Yahweh:

> And I will stretch forth my hand against Judah,
> and against the inhabitants of Jerusalem;
> And I will cut off from this place the name of Baal
> and the remnant[4] of his priests (1:4).

Is it coincidental that one of the first acts of the youthful king was the destruction of the Baal images together with all the accoutrements of idolatry so fashionable at the time? Everywhere he looked, Zephaniah saw fodder for the judgment of the day of Yahweh. Most of it was prepared by the easy deviationists who could not distinguish between good and evil (1:12), who found life under pagan cult usages far more attractive than the stern moral requirements of Yahwism. It would be going a bit far to say that Josiah hoped to wipe out all Baalistic tendencies by destroying the external symbols of the cult; but it most assuredly marked a good beginning.

The extension of the purge noted above probably came about after the king had dealt with the idolatries of Judah and Jerusalem. His expedition to the north reflects the ambition of Josiah to be another David, taking advantage of the ambivalent character of world politics at the time—the period between the decline of Assyria and the rise of the neo-Babylonian empire as the dominant world power. His zeal to emulate his great ancestor manifested itself in both political and religious aspects. He was joined by the Yahwist priests and prophets; indeed he may have been inspired by them. And the momentum with which he began his purge was maintained throughout his reign. In later years it got out of hand and cost him his life.

If Josiah was to be successful in his venture, something more than a negative approach was essential. Like his model David, he carried forward his concerns by taking a strong hand in the rehabilitation of the temple whose worship had become corrupt during the reigns of his immediate predecessors. Both Kings and Chronicles assert that for some time, perhaps between the eighth and eighteenth years of Josiah's reign, funds were being gathered to make the necessary repairs to the temple. In the eighteenth

year, Josiah sent Shaphan, his secretary, to the high priest Hilkiah
with the order to begin the work of temple restoration. In the
course of that transaction, Hilkiah reported the finding of a
sēpher hattôrāh (book of the torah) in the house of Yahweh which
he gave to Shaphan. After reading it, he returned to the king and
informed him that the work on the temple was in progress. He
then told him of Hilkiah's book which he read before the king
whose reaction indicated profound chagrin. Josiah ordered his
council to consult the Lord immediately "concerning the words
of the book" (2 Kings 22:13; 2 Chron. 34:21). They brought the
matter to the attention of Huldah, the prophetess—another indication of the loyalty of some to Yahweh during the preceding
dark years. In essence, she responded in virtually the same tenor
as Zephaniah did a little earlier. The wrath of Yahweh had been
aroused against "this place and its inhabitants" because of their
apostasy, "and it shall not be quenched." There was no mitiga-
tion of the purpose of Yahweh for land and people but because
the king had humbled himself and become penitent he would
be spared. Both sources agree substantially on Huldah's prophecy.

That the sequence of events is somewhat schematized in Kings
and Chronicles is beyond question, as Bright[5] and the commentators have pointed out, but the general course as outlined above
is certainly not beyond credibility. The early reforming activity
was in progress when the torah book turned up. It is altogether
possible that the king and his advisers were not fully aware of the
national deprivation until the warnings of the torah book were
substantiated by the live oracle of Huldah. It was apparent to them
then that nothing short of a national revival of the covenant
could save Judah. Josiah took the bull by the horns. He summoned the elders of Judah and Jerusalem who doubtless spread
the alarm, for presently they, with all the people of Judah and
Jerusalem, including priests and prophets, went up to the temple
to listen to "all the words of the book of the covenant" (2 Kings
23:2; 2 Chron. 34:30). While the general reaction of all who
heard it is not disclosed immediately, it is said after the cove-
nanting ceremony that "all the people stood by the covenant"
(2 Kings 23:3). The Chronicler is more pointed: "Then he made
all who were found in Jerusalem and Benjamin to stand [by the
covenant]" (2 Chron. 34:32a). After the reading of the book,
Josiah "stood in his place and made a covenant before Yahweh

46

to follow Yahweh, to keep his commandments and his testimonies and his stipulations with his whole heart and soul, to carry out the words of this covenant that are written in this book" (2 Kings 23:3). In this verse the term *berith* (covenant) is used in two different ways. The covenant made by Josiah amounts to a promise to abide by the terms of the book. The second use of covenant is more original because it obviously refers to Yahweh's offer made to Israel. In the first instance it was the king who made the covenant for himself and his people, really a solemn vow of acceptance of the stipulations of the torah book. The torah book itself represents Yahweh's direction for his people and must refer back to the Sinai-Horeb event.[6]

What transpired after the solemnizing of the covenant was apparently a continuation of the reformation begun earlier but, according to the author of 2 Kings, carried on with greater zeal. Once more, this was the king's and nation's response to Yahweh, an attempt to follow his direction for ridding the land of the idolatrous rubbish that had accumulated. This kind of action had a different motive and direction from that which involved Israel after the deliverance from Egypt. Insofar as the Kings narrative is concerned, it appears to be set in a framework of repentance and amendment of the life of people and nation in order to avert catastrophe. The aim of the reformation was the salvation of a nation that had forgotten the grace and goodness of Yahweh to the fathers, that had abandoned the moral direction or instruction of Yahweh revealed to Moses and the prophets, that had, in the words of Jeremiah, "changed their Glory for what is worthless" (2:11), and that had lost all sense of value. Persistence in going that way could only lead to self-annihilation. That was the view of the Deuteronomic historian supported by the Chronicler.

B. THE BOOK OF DEUTERONOMY

It has already been hinted that the torah book of Josiah was not our present book of Deuteronomy. There are numerous views as to the content of the torah book[7] but it is generally agreed that it included chapters 12–26, 28–30. The introductory chapters 1–11; 27; and the epilogue, 31–34 were, in all probability excluded from the torah book. However, it did perhaps contain some sort of preamble. There may also be some later additions in the main body of the torah book as Eissfeldt thought.[8]

The first thing to note is that the book of Deuteronomy forms part of a vast historical corpus extending through 2 Kings[9] that relates Israel's history from Moses to the exile of Judah from the point of view of its author-compiler. Like much of Israel's literature, Deuteronomy is tendentious, its chief aim being to convince the nation of sin to the point of repentance, i.e., the maintenance of the covenant.[10] Though the Josianic reformation was, in essence, legislation by covenant, the book of Deuteronomy as it now stands partakes of the old structure and form though it provides a different setting. It is presented basically as response literature. While it embodies much of the Book of the Covenant (Exod. 20–23) which it means to replace,[11] its historical introduction (1:1–4:40) places the scene far away from Sinai-Horeb, i.e., on the border of the promised land. The so-called first speech of Moses reviews the movements of Israel from Sinai-Horeb to "the other side of the Jordan"—the plains of Moab, the stage upon which the scenario is played out. It ends with an impassioned plea for Israel "to observe the stipulations and judgments" which Yahweh had given them through Moses (4:1–40) with the solemn reminder that "Yahweh your God is a consuming fire, a jealous God" (4:26). The main stress in this address falls on Yahweh's *berîth* (covenant) which is equated with "these ten words."

Beginning with 4:44 and running to 11:32 appears a second introduction to the main code, perhaps the more relevant of the two to the compiler.[12] Throughout there runs emphasis on the current situation to which the writer speaks. The binding nature of the Sinai-Horeb torah with its elaboration and application is striking. "Yahweh our God made a covenant with us at Horeb; it was not (only) with our fathers that Yahweh made this covenant, but with ourselves, with those of us who are all here alive today" (5:2–3). The speaker always has one eye on the past, the other on the present. He accentuates the torah element throughout as may be seen from the frequent occurrence of the term *šāmar* (to keep, observe, take care to) as if to point out that current troubles in the nation were due to Judah's failure to fulfill its covenant promises. "O that their present attitude (i.e., the attitude of allegiance reflected by the peoples' awe) might lead them always to stand in awe of me and keep all my commands, that it might go well with them and with their children for all time" (5:29), laments Yahweh. That is why they were to do as

48

enjoined in the *Shema'* (6:4–9) on the basis of what Yahweh had done for them (6:20–25). It was a cogent reminder that Israel had so often forgotten its heritage. The reference to the blessing and curse set before Israel (11:26 ff.) is reminiscent of chapter 27 and the Shechem covenant renewal of Joshua 24.

We are not so much concerned with the Deuteronomic covenant forms—that has been done by others[13]—but rather with the concept of Yahweh's grace and instruction (torah). Hillers' chapter on "The Old Age of an Idea"[14] has grasped the fundamental significance of the covenant principles as originally conceived and adapted to a later situation. There is no need here to discuss the origin of the code, for it is not a question as to where it came from but rather how it was used at the time of its compilation. The same pattern obtains here as in the earlier materials in Exodus. As observed above, the history of the tradition was received without substantive alteration. The preamble to the second discourse of Moses presents the historical milieu (4:44–5:5) which is followed immediately by the "ten words," complete with introductory formula but at the same time adaptation of several of them to the broader needs of the time (as in the Sabbath word). The original covenant code had no conditions attached to it, but admonitions.[15] The D-code begins in the same way: "I, Yahweh, am your God, who brought you up out of the land of Egypt, from the house of slaves" (5:6). Then it proceeds in like manner as the Exodus account. In the position which it now occupies in Deuteronomy, the covenant code serves as a motivating feature for what amounts to a covenantal renewal.

The theme of deliverance from Egyptian bondage occurs sixteen times, five of them (13:5, 10; 15:15; 24:18; 26:5b–9) in the code itself—a significant testimony to the continued basis of Israel's covenant fellowship with Yahweh who had saved them so signally. Along with this theme is that of Yahweh's care of and provision for his people in the wilderness. "You must remember all the experiences through which Yahweh your God has led you for the past forty years in the wilderness" (8:2). That is a central topic in the Song of Moses (32:10–14). In the first speech of Moses it is said, "he looked after you in your journey in this great wilderness; for forty years now Yahweh your God has been with you; you lacked nothing" (2:7). The conquest of Sihon and Og was accomplished by Yahweh (2:26–3:11) and his power alone. What

Yahweh did for helpless Israel was due to his election or choice of this people. Driver has noted that the idea of Yahweh's choice or election of Israel is "very characteristic of Deuteronomy: not applied before to God's choice of Israel."[16]

It is the motive for that choice that is of importance for our discussion. Yahweh's dealings with Israel were rooted and grounded in love. "Because he loved ('āhab) our fathers, and chose their descendants, and in his own person brought you out of Egypt by his great power, by driving out of your way nations greater and stronger than you, that he might bring you into a position to give you their land for a heritage . . ." (4:37–38). "It was not because you were the greatest of all peoples that Yahweh set his heart (ḥāšaq) on you and chose you—for you were the smallest of all peoples—but it was because Yahweh loved (mē'ahabat yhwh) you, and wanted to keep the oath he swore to your fathers . . ." (7:7–8). "Although the heavens to the highest heavens belong to Yahweh your God, and the earth with all that is in it, Yahweh became attached to (ḥāšaq) your fathers so as to love (le'aḥābāh) them, and chose their descendants, even you, in preference to all peoples" (10:14–15). That love and attachment would continue (7:13) from Yahweh's side. Those quotations illustrate the unconditional love of Yahweh for his people which the Deuteronomist is at pains to stress again and again in the hope of motivating the people of his day to respond in kind.[17] The root for love ('hb) occurs some twenty-three times in our book, and only here in the Pentateuch of God's love for his people. That is the fundamental doctrine of the prophecy of Hosea; which doubtless influenced the compiler and/or author of Deuteronomy.

The gracious love of God for his people was employed by the writer of our book to argue for a favorable response on the part of the people. Such great love ought not go unrequited. Simply because Yahweh is a merciful God (4:31; 13:18; 30:3) his people do not have license to flout his will or disregard his instruction (torah). The author of 1 John may have had Deuteronomy in mind: "We love, because he first loved us" (4:19) and "Beloved, if God so loved us, we also ought to love one another" (4:11). That is in essence the theme of Deuteronomy. But how is the people of Yahweh to respond to his love? Quite simply by being his people, as expressed by Jeremiah: "I will be your God, and you shall be my people" (7:23). Deuteronomy spells out in detail, for the time, the qualifications of the people of God, not beyond comprehension or impossible of realization. "For this charge which I am enjoining on you today is not beyond your power, nor is it out of reach; it is not in the heavens, that you should say, 'O that someone would ascend to the heavens for us, and get to know it for us, and then relay it to us, so that we may observe it!' Nor is it beyond the sea, that you should say, 'Oh that someone would cross the sea for us, and then relay it to us, so that we may observe it!' No, the matter is very near you, on your mouth and in your mind, for you to observe" (30:11–14). Not only were the people conceived of as having the power to requite God's love, but they had the prerogative to choose for themselves whether to obey or disobey, to fulfill their destiny as God's people or to reject it. "Behold, I set before you today life and prosperity, along with death and adversity . . . therefore choose life, that you as well as your descendants may live, by loving Yahweh your God, by heeding his injunctions, and by holding fast to him" (30:15, 19b–20a).

Space permits the presentation of only a few of the major directions by which Yahweh's people may express their love for him in very practical and concrete ways. The first, and perhaps paramount, direction has to do with the maintenance of faith in Yahweh as the sole God, the one who delivered the nation from Egypt and graciously gave her a torah. One method of manifesting and strengthening that faith and maintaining its undiluted quality was to provide one sanctuary in the place which Yahweh chooses. A major reason for the predicament in which the nation found itself at the time, according to the code of Deuteronomy, was the persistence of Baalistic vestiges at many local high places. The Deuteronomist promoted the famous creed (6:6) of Yahweh as the one God. There were not many Yahwehs; since Yahweh was one, worship of him could be legitimized at only one place. Throughout the entire book, there is the ever-insistent warning against alien gods (5:7; 6:14; 7:4; 8:19; 11:16, 28; 13:2, 6; 17:3; 18:20; 28:14, 36, 64; 29:26; 30:17; 31:18, 20). The only way, they believed, to overcome the temptation was to keep worship under close surveillance which could best be achieved at one sanctuary. But the matter does not stop there. There must be faithful worship at that one sanctuary: "there you must go, and there bring your burnt offerings, your sacrifices, your dues, your personal contributions, your votive offerings, your voluntary offerings, and the firstlings of your herd and flock; and there you must eat before Yahweh your God, and with your households rejoice over all your undertakings, in which Yahweh your God has blessed you" (12:6, 7). The annual contributions must be brought to the sanctuary (14:22 ff.). Three times a year every male must come to appear before Yahweh (16:16 f.) and the passover is no longer to be celebrated away from the sanctuary (16:5 ff.).

Deuteronomy, like other areas of the Old Testament, conceived of horizontal relationships as well as a vertical one. Love for God could not be sharply differentiated from love for one's fellows. There were to be no poor among the people (15:4), i.e., provision was to be made in all sorts of ways to alleviate the needs of those who may have fallen upon hard times. That is why there was to be a year of release (15:1–2), why those who had to sell themselves into slavery had to be released from service in the seventh year (15:12 ff.). Judges and magistrates must deal fairly and honestly with the people; justice must not be perverted, or partiality shown, or bribery resorted to (16:18–20). Magic, sorcery, and false prophets must not be allowed to mislead the gullible. Family matters, too, were of paramount concern to the nation (22:13 ff.), as were those of health and safety (22:8). Of course these and other facets of community life, earlier enforced only by religious sanction, were now given the endorsement of the king by virtue of *his* covenant with Yahweh (2 Kings 23:3). But the very presence of the curse chapter (27) and the beautifully balanced blessings and curses in 28 still point to the writer's hope of enforcement by the freewill choice of the people for a Yahweh-people relationship based on reciprocal love. If the covenant is observed, i.e., if the nation's love for Yahweh is maintained, then

> "Blessed will you be in the city,
> And blessed will you be in the country;
> Blessed will be the fruit of your body,
> The fruit of your soil and the fruit of live-stock,
> The offspring of your cattle and lambing of your flocks;
> Blessed will be your basket and your kneading-trough;
> Blessed will be your coming,
> And blessed will be your going" (28:3–6).

On the other hand, if covenant-love is not maintained, then

"Cursed will you be in the city,
And cursed will you be in the country;
Cursed will be your basket and your kneading-trough;
Cursed will be the fruit of your body and the fruit of your soil,
The offspring of your cattle and the lambing of your flocks;
Cursed will be your coming,
And cursed will be your going" (28:16–19).

C. THE PROPHETS

Most of the seventh century prophets approach Deuteronomy from a somewhat different direction. There is parallel terminology, to be sure, though the main thrust varies, especially from that evident in Josiah's reformation which was enforced by the king. These prophets hark back to the Exodus pattern, criticizing the nation for its failure to respond to Yahweh's gracious acts of redemption and preservation. Judah was worse than Samaria (Ezek. 23:11), even doting on her wickedness.

1. Jeremiah

The greatest of the seventh-sixth century prophets has much in common with Hosea. Covenantal language abounds in Jeremiah's oracles and throughout the book that bears his name. Whether "this covenant" in 11:2, 3, 6 refers to the Josianic covenant or the Mosaic covenant is uncertain.[18] The language is Deuteronomic, and perhaps not too much ought to be made of it, but the whole passage laments Judah's half-hearted performance of its vows no matter which covenant may be involved. There may have been a formal acceptance of its provisions, as chapters 7 and 26 indicate, but the heart of the people was not in it. It was not too demanding to carry out the worship provisions; it was far more difficult to implement its social and moral objectives which, in the prophets' view were far more important. To observe the letter was easier and more attractive than to be dominated by its spirit. Faith in Yahweh is a matter of the whole life of the people, not merely the observance of festivals and processions. To be Yahweh's people meant a genuine reflection of his character not only in their dealings with him but also in their dealings with one another in social, economic, and political relationships. What Jeremiah had in mind all along is illustrated in the pledge to release slaves and the subsequent reneging on that pledge (34:8–22). That is why he spoke of a "new covenant" which would be written on the hearts, i.e., motivate the springs of action. In place of sin engraved on their hearts (17:1) will be "my torah" put within them, written on their hearts.

The content of the covenant remains the same. What is to be written on the hearts of the people is "my torah." Detailed description of the torah ingredients are given in the temple sermon: honest dealings with one another, supporting the cause of the alien, the orphan, and the widow, refraining from shedding innocent blood in this place and from idolatry (7:5b–6). One of the chief caveats of Jeremiah was the warning against the following of the *lo' 'elōhīm* (the no-gods) (2:11). Most of the first sermon of the prophet deals with apostasy (2:1–4:4). If further proof is necessary to establish the fact that the old torah was recalled by him, it is to be found in 7:9—"What? Steal, murder, commit adultery, swear falsely," a clear reminiscence of the Decalogue. Then there is a profusion of references to deliverance from Egypt which precedes the gift of the torah (2:6, 7:22, 25; 11:4, 7; 16:14; 23:7; 31:32; 32:20–22; 34:13). In nearly all of those passages emphasis falls on deliverance and the subsequent covenant which was not observed by Israel except in the breach.

Other covenant terms are not lacking in Jeremiah. Yahweh is referred to as being true (*'emeth*) in 10:10 and 32:41, i.e., he can be depended upon to do what he promised. Jeremiah speaks of Israel's loyalty and devotion in the early days (2:2), but more often of Yahweh's loyalty (*ḥesed*). In 9:23 he asserts:

> "Now I, Yahweh, practice loyalty,
> Justice, and righteousness on the earth."

The same quality is attributed to him in 16:5. In the Book of Consolation (30–33), the prophet proclaims future hope for Israel because

> "With an everlasting love *'aḥabat 'ōlām*) have I loved you
> (*'aḥabtīka*)
> Therefore with devotion (*ḥesed*) will I draw you to me" (31:3).

After handing over the deed for the purchase of the patrimony from Hanamel to Baruch, Jeremiah prays to Yahweh affirming Yahweh's showing "devotion" to thousands (32:18). In 33:10 (in the Hebrew 33:11) there is apparently a quotation from a Psalm:

"Give thanks to Yahweh of hosts,
For Yahweh is good (*ṭôb*)
For his loyalty (*ḥasdo*) is eternal."

Only once is there mention in Jeremiah of Yahweh's love (31:3) for Israel and that in the framework of restoration and in the context of a continuing concern for his people Israel. The strong Deuteronomic emphasis on love as the basis for election is wanting.[19] As a matter of fact, the root '*hb* occurs only thirteen times in the whole book and mostly in normal meanings. Why this should be is not apparent, though it may have been because of the persistence of Baalism (2:20, 26; 3:2–6, 13). However, Jeremiah did employ *yāda'* (to know) in the convenantal sense,[20] though not in the explicit sense of Amos 3:2. He was aware of a special relationship to Yahweh as may be seen from 1:5—"Before I formed you in the womb I knew you," i.e., set apart as Yahweh's special messenger. While the prophet recognized Yahweh's summons, that he was a man under contractual orders, Israel failed to take seriously its call as his people. "It is because my people is stupid, and they do not know me" (4:22; cf. also 9:3, 6); they do not realize their torah responsibility and blithely follow their own ways with no conception of what their position vis-à-vis Yahweh entailed. In a scathing attack on Jehoiakim, Jeremiah bursts out

"Did not your father, as he ate and drank,
Do justice and righteousness?
So it went well with him.
The cause of the poor and needy he defended—
Then it went well.
Is not that how to know (*hadda'at*) me?" (22:15b–16).

When the new covenant is inscribed on their hearts, "all of them shall know (*yēdᵉ'ū*) me, from the least of them to the greatest of them" (31:34). They will be invested with motivation to respond to Yahweh's overtures in thanksliving!

2. Ezekiel

The classical covenantal language is wanting in Ezekiel. There is a reference to "the covenant with you in the days of your youth" in 16:60.[21] There is another unmistakable reminiscence, though the term is absent, in the following passage: "On the day that I chose Israel, and swore an oath (lit. = lifted up my hand) to the family of Jacob—revealing myself to them in the land of Egypt, and swearing an oath to them saying, 'I am Yahweh your God'—on that day I swore an oath to them, that I would bring them out of the land of Egypt to a land that I had given to them, a land flowing with milk and honey, a land which is the glory of all lands; and I said to them, 'cast away each one the detestable things which you love, and do not defile yourselves with the idols of Egypt; I am Yahweh your God.' But they rebelled against me, and refused to listen to me . . ." (20:5–8). These are the only direct references to Egyptian bondage and deliverance therefrom in the book. Even the term torah does not seem to have the same significance (it occurs only six times) as in the other prophets except perhaps in 22:26. It is true that the promise of restoration in 16:60, 62 postulates the establishment of an everlasting covenant which presupposed one that was not everlasting. Even the heart transplant in chapter 11 makes no mention of a covenant, though it does reiterate the covenantal formula of Jeremiah— "They shall be my people and I will be their God" (v. 20). "I will give them a new heart, and will put a new spirit within them; I will remove the heart of stone from their flesh and will give them a heart of flesh, so that they may follow my statutes (*ḥuqqōth*) and keep my judgments (*mishpāṭīm*)" (11:19).

In place of *ḥesed*,[22] *ᵉmeth, daᶜath* are *ḥuqqîm-ḥuqqōth* (stipulations) and *mishpāṭīm* (judgments).[23] Ezekiel, a priest himself, is strongly influenced by the priestly line of thought and action. In his accusation of Jerusalem, the prophet says: "I set her in the midst of the nations, with lands round about her. Yet she wickedly rebelled against my stipulations and judgments . . . for her people have scorned my judgments and failed to observe my stipulations . . ." (5:6 ff.). One feels that what is involved here is the prophet's accentuation of the priestly torah rather than the broad principles of direction of the "ten words" or even the book of the covenant, though the terms occur in the latter. The *ḥuqqōth* are prescribed decrees which must be obeyed rather than directions for response to divine deliverance from bondage. Professor Georg Fohrer has written that "Ezekiel does not have to do with an objective attestation of the works of God but with the proper behavior of man and the responsive reaction of God."[24] The almost pathosless character of Ezekiel determines his conception of Yahweh and Israel. Israel had violated his covenant (= almost law) and thus debauched his honor. What Yahweh demands is conformity to his will, the lack of which demands retribution. As Kuhl has pointed out, "The motive for Yahweh's gracious guidance of His people in spite of their disobedience and rebellion and for His promised deliverance is not, as in Hosea, His love for His people, but 'it is not for your sake, O house of Israel, that I am about to act, but for the sake of My holy name.' "[25] The crucial expressions of Ezekiel are the $k^ebōd$ Yahweh (the glory of Yahweh) and that "they may know that I am Yahweh." The overriding message of Ezekiel is that the salvation of Israel, as well as the punishment of other nations and recalcitrant Israelites, is for the glory of Yahweh and the display of his glory and majesty among the nations. Ezekiel's God is thus one of majesty whose major concern is the maintenance of his position, by virtue of which he exercises judgment of condemnation and salvation.

3. Isaiah 40–66

Eichrodt[26] has said that the interpretation of the covenant concept reached its zenith in these chapters of the book of Isaiah. That is surely so, inasmuch as it is conceived as having universal significance and in the so-called servant poems there is actually the pattern of what a true respondent to the covenant is and does. The term covenant ($b^erîth$) occurs six times but not in the old Sinaitic sense. The old, only a shadow of things to come, will be replaced by an everlasting covenant, a common term in the P document, (55:3; 61:8) of peace (54:10). In 42:6 and 48:9 the servant is spoken of as a people-covenant, i.e., as a bond of union, mediator, between Yahweh and the people. However, the Exodus terminology of deliverance is reflected in a number of passages.

> "Thus said Yahweh,
> Who made a way through the sea,
> A path through the mighty waters;
> Who led out chariot and horse,
> A powerful army mobilized—
> They lay down never to rise up,
> They were put out, extinguished like a wick.
>
> . . . .
>
> Moreover, I will make a highway in the wilderness,
> And rivers [paths—IQIsa] in the desert.
>
> . . . .

As I provided water in the wilderness,
And rivers in the desert,
To give drink to my chosen people" (43:19, 20).

"They did not thirst when I led them through the deserts,
He made water to flow from the rock for them;
He cleft the rock and water gushed out" (48:21).

The same reminiscence is reflected in 51:9–13 (cf. also 50:2). 52:4 views the exile as a second sojourn in Egypt (cf. also 43:4; 63:11). Kurt Galling[27] saw in 52:11 ff. the flight from Babylon, a parallel to that from Egypt.

The concept of election is quite prominent. Jacob-Israel is Yahweh's chosen one, his servant (41:8, 9) who needs not fear because Yahweh is his God (44:1 ff.). But election here is not to privilege as such, though Israel still has some preference, but for service. The most significant passage is 43:10:

" 'You are my witnesses,' oracle of Yahweh,
My servants, whom I have chosen—
That you may know (*tēde'ū*) and believe (*ta'amînu*) me,
And understand that I am he.' "

A remarkable piece, referred to by commentators as the second Cyrus song (44:5–9) but regarded by some as an appendix to the first servant poem.[28] It is by no means certain, however, that the oracle is addressed to the servant of Yahweh who is "clearly an individual servant,"[29] which is the basis for thinking of it as a Cyrus poem. It is essential to quote here the salient verses of the poem and then show how the covenant was thought of by the author.

I, Yahweh, have summoned you in righteousness,
And I have taken you by the hand;
I have created you and made you a people-covenant,—
A light in the nations—
To open the eyes of the blind,
To bring out prisoners from the dungeon,
Those who dwell in darkness from confinement" (42:6–7).[30]

The language of Hos. 11:6 ff. is unmistakable here. The universalism of the prophet is evident. Not only is the one addressed to be delivered but he is himself to be a people-covenant to others. Again the idea of service stands out in the election of the person or community addressed. The vast experience of Israel ought to make the people more susceptible now to the call of Yahweh. They were blind and deaf, they had seen much but learned nothing, they had heard much but to no avail. Yahweh hoped they would accept his grand and glorious torah but their life showed they had not done so. Hence they had been plundered and spoiled, herded into caves, thrust into dungeons. Why? Because they had sinned, failed to walk in his ways, paid no attention to his torah. Having learned their lesson once more in exile in a second Egypt (Babylon), Yahweh again took them by the hand and reconstituted them to be the bearer of his torah (light) to the nations. They would become his word to mankind—a word of judgment and salvation, as the case might require. They are to be his witnesses (43:12), the people he created for himself to recount his praise (43:21). The theme is deliverance, response, and the torah of service.

Brief reference may be made here also to the fact that "Israel is saved by Yahweh, with an everlasting salvation" (45:17); "he became their deliverer in all their distress" (63:8b). The prophet, in 51:7, may echo the thought of Jer. 31:31 ff. What should be the response to the divine deliverance is expressed quite forcefully in 58:2, 6–7, 9b–12. Salvation followed by torah, service in accordance with Yahweh's direction, is the prime thrust of Isa. 40–66.[31]

4. Post-exilic Prophets

The post-exilic prophets follow, in general, the Deuternomic conceptions though with a slightly different prespective. Deuteronomy's covenantal observance was directed toward the sparing of the nation from disintegration and destruction. It did not succeed in achieving its basic purpose; it did, however, provide an outlook upon the divine-human (Israelite) relationship that influenced so much later life and thought. The problems were, of course, different but Deuteronomy had something of more than passing value to offer.

For the prophets after the exile the problem was survival of the restored community in the midst of the most trying circumstances. The diagnosis of the situation given by both Haggai and Zechariah (1–8) is the same—neglect of the religious institutions. That too was one of the major concerns of Deuteronomy. Haggai says virtually nothing about the religio-moral life of the people.

He does stress the promise of Yahweh to be with Zerubbabel and Jehozadak in accordance with the announcement to the people of the exodus but the idea of torah as response is totally lacking.[32] While Zechariah too emphasizes the necessity for institutional restoration (1:16; 4:9, 14), he calls attention to preachments of "the former prophets" (1:4; 7:12) which are referred to as "the torah and the words which Yahweh of hosts sent by his spirit through the former prophets." There is some other covenant terminology in Zechariah. Yahweh will again choose (*bāḥar*) Jerusalem (1:17; 2:16 (12 in Eng.); 3:2) and the prophet urges response thereto by "rendering true judgments (*mishpāṭ 'emeth*), do *ḥesed* and mercy (*raḥamim*) each toward his brother" (7:9). Here are echoes of the early tradition. Joel (ca. 500 B.C.) likewise calls for repentance and true fasting (2:12b) because Yahweh is gracious (*ḥannūn*) and merciful (*raḥḥūm*), slow to anger and plenteous in *ḥesed* (2:13). But note that repentance precedes the graciousness of Yahweh. The word *berîth* (covenant) occurs six times in Malachi. Once it has to do with the marriage contract (2:14). Three times (2:4, 5, 8) it refers to "the covenant with Levi" which Karl Elliger interprets as community relationship whose content is set forth in 1:6 f. and implies that God is the giver, man (the community) the recipient and respondent.[33] Here the old covenant conception is maintained. The "covenant of our fathers" (2:10) is doubtless Deuteronomic in reference. Just what "the messenger of the covenant" means is unclear.[34]

On the whole, therefore, those prophets are vitally concerned with the national or, better, community stiuation in their time. Once again existence hung in the balance and the same cure is advised that prevailed for the Deuteronomists—institutional rehabilitation and obedience to the torah. Gone for the most part are the threats and punishments of the earlier prophets because they are already operative in the misfortunes of the time. The chief interest of the religious leaders is how to deal with them. The solution: restoration of proper and acceptable worship and the practice of covenant relationships in the community. Yahweh's love is still operative but remains unrequited (Mal. 1:2).

NOTES

1. This is especially significant if we assume two Assyrian campaigns in the west, one in 701 B.C. as reported in the Taylor Prism of Sennacherib

(cf. Pritchard, *ANET*, pp. 287 f.) and another ca. 688 B.C. For detailed discussion of the problem see J. Bright, *A History of Israel* (Philadelphia: Westminster Press, 1959), pp. 282–287.

2. Cf. A. T. Olmstead, *History of Palestine and Syria* (New York: Scribner, 1931), chap. 32.

3. This passage has been viewed with undue skepticism. See my *II Chronicles* (New York: Doubleday, 1965), p. 205 f. and Y. Aharoni, *The Land of the Bible* (Philadelphia: Westminster Press, 1967), p. 349.

4. Interchanging *sm* (name) and *s'r* (remnant), partly with LXX. The symbolism used here doubtless covers all vestiges of idolatry with its consequences and not just Baalism in particular. Cf. Charles Venn Pilcher, *Three Hebrew Prophets* (London: Religious Tract Society, 1931), p. 156.

5. *Op. cit.*, pp. 295–297; John Gray, *I & II Kings* (Philadelphia: Westminster Press, 1963), pp. 649 ff.; James A. Montgomery and Henry S. Gehman, *The Books of the Kings* (New York: Scribner, 1951), pp. 523 ff., especially the additional note to II, 22–23:30, pp. 541 ff.

6. The so-called code of Deuteronomy must have had some kind of introduction; it could hardly have begun with 12:1. Cf. John Gray, *op cit.*, p. 652. On the significance of Josiah's act and its peculiar nature see Delbert R. Hiller's *Covenant: The History of a Biblical Idea* (Baltimore: The Johns Hopkins Press, 1969), p. 146b; and G. E. Mendenhall, "Covenant" in *IDB*, 1:721; and *Law and Covenant in Israel and the Ancient Near East,* p. 21.

7. Since the days of St. Jerome it was regarded as containing the nucleus of Deuteronomy. Consult the commentaries on Kings and Chronicles and the standard introductions to the Old Testament.

8. Otto Eissfeldt, *The Old Testament: An Introduction* (New York: Harper & Row, 1965), p. 226 f.

9. See M. Noth, *Überlieferungsgeschichtliche Studien,* 2nd ed. (Tübingen: Niemeyer, 1957), pp. 3–110; G. von Rad, *Studies in Deuteronomy* (London: SCM Press, 1953).

10. On Deuteronomy and the covenant see D. J. McCarthy, *Old Testament Covenant* (Oxford: Basil Blackwell, 1972), p. 22 f. and *Treaty and Covenant* (Rome: PBI, 1963), pp. 109–140. Barnabas Lindars, "Torah in Deuteronomy" in *Words and Meanings: Essays Presented to David Winton Thomas,* ed. Peter R. Ackroyd and Barnabas Lindars (Cambridge: Cambridge University Press, 1968), pp. 117–136, esp. pp. 129 ff.

11. For an outline of duplicates between the two see G. von Rad's "Deuteronomy" in *IDB*, 1:832 f., especially Table I; and S. R. Driver *An Introduction to the Literature of the Old Testament* (New York: Scribner, 1913), pp. 73–75, also in tabular form; and *Deuteronomy,* pp. iv–vii.

12. On the place of this section see S. R. Driver, *Deuteronomy* (New York: Scribner, 1912), pp. lxv–lxvi.

13. See Klaus Baltzer, *The Covenant Formulary* (Philadelphia: Fortress Press, 1971), pp. 31–38; D. J. McCarthy, *Treaty and Covenant,* pp. 109–140; D. J. McCarthy, *Old Testament Covenant,* pp. 22–23, 67–72; Delbert R. Hillers, *Covenant,* pp. 143–168; W. Eichrodt, *Theology of the Old Testament* (Philadelphia: Westminster Press, 1961), 1:52 ff.

14. See preceding note.

15. D. J. McCarthy, *Treaty and Covenant*, p. 111.

16. *Deuteronomy*, p. lxxx. Cf. W. F. Albright, *History, Archaeology and Christian Humanism* (New York: McGraw-Hill, 1964), pp. 281 f.

17. McCarthy has well said that "it is the occasion for a profound theology of grace and love, providence and much else" (*Treaty and Covenant*, p. 117). See further W. L. Moran, "The Ancient Near Eastern Background of the Love of God in Deuteronomy," *CBQ*, 25 (1963): 77–87.

18. See John Bright, *Jeremiah* (New York: Doubleday, 1965), p. 89. On the theological usage of the term *berîth* see A. Jepsen, "Berith: Ein Beitrag zur Theologie der Exilszeit" in *Verbannung und Heimkehr* (Tübingen: J. C. B. Mohr [Paul Siebeck], 1961), pp. 161–179.

19. See note 17.

20. See H. B. Huffman, "The Treaty Background of Hebrew Yāda'," *BASOR* 181 (Feb. 1966): 31–37, esp. p. 36, and Hillers, *op. cit.*, pp. 122 ff.

21. On the whole passage see W. Eichrodt, *Ezekiel* (Philadelphia: Westminster, 1970), pp. 216–220; W. Zimmerli, *Ezechiel* (BKAT, XIII, 5) (Neukirchen: Neukirchener Verlag, 1958), pp. 369–371 and 62 f.; W. Eichrodt, *Theology of the Old Testament*, 1:59–61.

22. See Zimmerli, *Ezechiel*, p. 34.

23. On the meaning of these categories see A. Alt, *Essays on Old Testament History and Religion* (New York: Doubleday Anchor Books, 1968), pp. 117 and 159; and Zimmerli, *Ezechiel*, p. 133 f., "Jerusalem's transgression is not something vague but violation of clearly revealed divine law." On the concept of "the covenant of peace" (34:25; 37:26) see M. Noth, "Das alttestamentliche Bundschliessen im Lichte eines Mari-Textes" in *Mélanges Isidore Levy* (Brussels :Annuaire de l'institut de philologie et d'histoire orientales et slaves, vol. 13 (1953, 1955): 433–444.

24. *Ezechiel* (Tübingen: J. C. B. Mohr, [Paul Siebeck], 1955), p. xxvi.

25. *The Prophets of Israel* (Richmond: John Knox Press, 1960), p. 129.

26. *Op. cit.*, p. 63.

27. "Von Naboned zu Darius" in *ZDPV*, 70 (1954): 25.

28. Cf. C. R. North, *The Suffering Servant in Deutero-Isaiah* (London: Oxford University Press, 1948), pp. 131–135; P.-E. Dion, "Les chants du Serviteur de Yahweh." *Biblica*, 51 (1970): 28–31.

29. Dion, *ibid.*, p. 28.

30. Cf. the interpretation of the Targum on the passage.

31. For significant observations on *ṣedāqāh* and the covenant in Isa. 40–66, see Father J. J. Scullion, "Ṣedeq-Ṣedaqah in Isaiah cc. 40–66" in *Ugarit-Forschungen*, 3 (Neukirchen-Vluyn: Verlag Butzon & Bercker Kevelaer, 1971): 335–348, esp. pp. 341, 344, 348; and now John L. McKenzie, *A Theology of the Old Testament* (New York: Doubleday & Co., 1974), p. 154.

32. The one occurrence of the term in 2:11 refers to a priestly decision.

33. *Das Alte Testament Deutsch 25 Die Propheten: Nahum, Habakuk, Zephanja, Haggai, Zacharja, Maleachi* (Göttingen: Vandenhoeck & Ruprecht, 1950), p. 185 f.

34. Cf. *ibid.*, p. 197.

IV

Salvation and Torah
in the New Testament

Klaus Baltzer[1] has made a good case for the use of the covenant formulary, with variations, in Jewish and early Christian texts. He calls attention to the desirability of an investigation of the structure of New Testament Epistles. The objective of this chapter is not to investigate that structure but to point out the broad conception of the general scheme observed in the Exodus and prophetic traditions which appears to be followed, perhaps unconsciously, by St. Paul in Romans and some others of his epistles.

A. A BRIEF SURVEY OF THE CONTENT AND ORDER OF ROMANS

It may be well to begin our study with a short account of just what the apostle says in his famous letter to the Romans and then take up his basic message. As usual, Paul begins with a greeting in which he sets forth his faith in Jesus Christ and his lordship (1:1–7), followed by the reason for this composition (1:8–15). In two short but significant verses he outlines the theme of his gospel which he defines as "the power of God for salvation to everyone who believes" (1:16–17). From here on, Romans is really an exposition of that subject. He asserts that without the gospel only the wrath of God is revealed against both heathen (1:18–32) and Jews (2:1–13). Though the heathen may have no written law, their hearts and consciences accuse them (2:14–16). The Jews do have it in writing and are proud of it but fail to obey it (2:17–29). Despite their failure on this point they do have a special advantage (3:1–2). Their unfaithfulness does not nullify the promises of God (3:3–8). But both Jews and heathen are guilty of sin (3:9–20) as the Scripture affirms. Now, however, the righteousness appropriated by faith has been made available to all who believe in redemption through Jesus Christ. Works no longer profit since

63

faith alone has merit before God (3:21–30). Nevertheless this does not mean invalidation of the law (3:31). The law already points in the direction of faith. Abraham was made righteous by faith and hence is a type for Christians (4:1–25). On grounds of this justification we have the certainty of future salvation (5:1–11). As once death came through Adam, so surely and universally will salvation come to mankind through Christ; yes, it will extend still further (5:12–21). Yet this fulness of divine grace does not allow us to do as we please (6:1). By baptism we have died with Christ, therefore after baptism we must live in Christ. Sin has been robbed of its power (6:2–14). We have been slaves of sin but now are slaves of righteousness (6:15–23). The first connubium with the law has been dissolved by death and now we belong to Christ (7:1–6). How? Is the law then to be equated with sin? The answer is, no. The law in itself is holy, but it makes sin manifest because the commandment awakens slumbering sin (7:7–13). The understanding approves the law but the flesh dwells in sin and is victorious in the struggle between them (7:14–26). But Christ has vanquished sin in the flesh and given us the Spirit who enables us to walk in righteousness (8:1–11). We must follow his guidance. That we already possess the Spirit is shown by our prayers (8:12–17). Thereby we have certain hope and prospect for future glory (8:18–25). We can be sure of salvation (8:26–39). Paul was a son of Israel and he was always troubled by the apparent rejection his people accorded to his gospel. So he devotes three chapters here to the problem. He asserts unequivocally that God has not abandoned Israel. God's promises remain firmly intact but they do not hold for corporeal Israel for which he has decreed obduracy. They apply to spiritual Israel which, according to God's inexplicable decree, he has predestined (9:1–23). The believing heathen too belong to the spiritual Israel (9:24–33), as the Scripture clearly affirms (10:1–15).

> "No one who believes in him shall be put to shame" (Isa. 28:16).

> "Everyone who calls upon the name of Yahweh will be saved" (Joel 2:32).

Nevertheless, Scripture also speaks of obdurate Israel (10:16–21). However, God has only temporarily blinded his people to the end

that the heathen may be saved (11:1–12). For that reason the wild
olive shoots who have been grafted into the genuine olive tree
must not boast over the branches. They must remember that it is
not the branches that support the root but the other way around
(11:13–24). In the end all Israel will be saved (11:25–36). The
hortatory section follows. The recipients were admonished to live
with a new discernment according to God's will. Their lives
must be harmonious and characterized by love (12:1–21). They
must be obedient to the governing authorities, love one another,
and so fulfill the law (13:1–10), because the parousia is at hand
(13:11–14). Those who are strong in the faith must welcome their
weak brothers, giving no offense to them (14:1–23). Let all follow the example of Christ (15:1–13). The letter closes with an
announcement of personal travel plans if matters turn out as
Paul hoped (15:14–32), and the usual benediction (15:33).

Detailed discussion of content is uncalled for here but it is of
vital importance to consider the order followed by the author of
Romans. E. J. Goodspeed, in his handbook on the New Testament,[2] began at the end of the letter to outline its thought and
then returned to a short discussion of 12:1–15:32, remarking that
this portion of the book is worthy of a place alongside of the Sermon on the Mount.[3] Had it not been put where it is, it might
have attracted more attention than is actually the case. "Here is,"
wrote Goodspeed, "a morality that does not grow old or obso-
lete."[4] Because they are more interested in minute doctrinal truth,
most modern commentators devote fewer pages to these chapters.[5]

The preceding chapters deal with a prior consideration upon
which the final chapters are contingent. Let us be clear about it:
this is not meant to be an abstruse doctrinal treatise; it is the
description of a quite concrete experience. As such it is couched
in what may be called factual, experiential terms. In broad outline, Paul follows the same general pattern found in the exodus
experience of the Old Testament.[6] He details the condition of
mankind in slavery to sin, in bondage to monstrous forces of evil
from which it was impossible to extricate itself by its own power
even if it had the will to do so. Deliverance was possible only
through the direct intervention of God in Christ. Because of his
great love and mercy, God did thus move to set man free and
gave him a new lease on life. Just as deliverance from the house
of slaves in Egypt was made evident by the departure of Israel

from the scenes of misery in Goshen, so is man's salvation made manifest by a new experience of freedom in Christ. How men were to respond to that deliverance is set forth in chapters 12–15. They were no longer slaves of sin but slaves of righteousness. Let us, therefore, examine more closely how the apostle deals with the problems of God's salvation in Christ and how he contemplates man's response thereto and then compare it with the Exodus model.

B. SLAVERY TO SIN AND DELIVERANCE THEREFROM

For our purpose indicated above, discussion here is limited to the first and last sections of Romans. Most commentators observe three distinct divisions of the book following the introduction. The first (1:18–8:39) deals with man's state of sin and God's gracious salvation in Christ; the second (9–11) discusses the place of Israel in Paul's scheme of God's redemption of all men; and the third (12–15) sketches man's state of grace in the Pauline milieu.

1. Man Enslaved by Sin (1:18–3:20).

After announcing that the gospel is "the power of God for salvation to everyone who believes, to the Jew first and also to the Greek" (1:16) Paul immediately launches into mankind's need for it. The whole world is in the clutches of sin and guilt as may be seen from the revelation of God's wrath. Man has invented all sorts of ways of escape but to no avail. These machinations only serve to expose his folly and desperation. Their wisdom turns out to be nonsense for they have succeeded only in exchanging "the glory of the immortal God for images resembling mortal man or birds or animals or reptiles" (1:23). Enslaved by sin, they reflected in life and action all the base characteristics of illicit passions and unbelievable wickedness: "They were filled with all manner of wickedness, evil, covetousness, malice. (They were) full of envy, murder, strife, deceit, malignity; they are gossipers, slanderers, haters of God, insolent, haughty, boastful, inventors of evil, disobedient to parents, foolish, faithless, heartless, ruthless" (1:29–31). What a catalogue of horrors of those caught in the toils of iniquity! Far worse than any Egyptian bondage and incalculably damaging to the soul. The situation Paul complains about has been confirmed in many contemporary documents.[7]

Because of the utter sinfulness of both Jew and Gentile, the judgment of God will assuredly fall upon them. Divine restraint, due to God's kindness and forebearance and patience, is intended to lead his people to repentance; but instead it has only hardened their hearts which is bound to arouse further the wrath of God who will show no partiality in judgment. Both Jew and Greek will receive their due reward, each judged by his own law—the former by the law of Moses, the latter by natural law and conscience. The Jew really has no advantage since the law accuses him but it has no inherent power to save or redeem him. Possession of the law does not confer any special favor on him; only the doing of it can avail. Mere possession of the law is no guarantee of salvation. The scales may tip in favor of the Jew who has the law but failure to live up to it and develop the highest kind of moral life renders him, in a sense, worse than those who do not have it. Calling to witness a series of Old Testament passages to substantiate his arguments Paul concludes that while the law is good and the Jews have been entrusted with the oracles of God, they are yet sinful as immoral conditions among them prove. The law, therefore, fails to justify; in fact it has made the situation even more disastrous by exhibiting their wrongdoing for all to see. It shows how immeasurably sinful sin is and how frightful is bondage thereto.

2. God's Response to Man's Plight (3:21–4:25).

Without divine intervention man's condition now is as hopeless and bleak as was Israel's in Pharaoh's house of slaves. God's righteousness has been manifested apart from the law, just as it was at the time of the exodus. Just how the expression "the righteousness of God" (3:21) is to be interpreted has been widely discussed without general agreement. It appears to the writer to have more of a covenantal significance[8] here than a legal or forensic one. Later on Paul employs the Abraham experience to prove his point; "Abraham believed God and it was reckoned to him for righteousness" (Gen. 15:6 and Rom. 4:3). In the Genesis context the same general situation pertains as in the Exodus story. Abraham responded to Yahweh's call and promise and that was reckoned as righteousness, i.e., the acceptance of his offer, an indication or expression of loyalty. The vindication of Abraham was more than a single act even of faith; it is marked by a host of movements summed up in Gen. 12:5—"they set out for the land of Canaan and to the land of Canaan they came." God's righteousness implies his gracious act of election-love and Abraham's righteousness represents his acceptance of God's designation and the decision to move in accordance with it. Trust was, of course, involved, just as it was in the exodus occasion.

Redemption in Christ was likewise a freely offered grace of God appropriated by faith and continued in faithfulness. Just as Israel had been enslaved by Egypt without hope of self-deliverance, so Paul asserts man to be enslaved by sin with no possibility of extrication except by the intervention of God himself. If man is not to become the victim of sin there must be some positive and effective move from God himself. This Paul says was done by Christ through his sacrifice. But whereas the exodus event was limited to a single people at a specific juncture in history, the Christ event, though it too occurred at a specific point in history, was effective for all time. Christ takes away the sin of the world and his salvation becomes available to all who believe, i.e., accept him and take advantage of his offer. "The words 'it was reckoned to him (i.e., Abraham) as righteousness,' were written not for his sake alone, but for ours also. It will be reckoned to us who believe in him that raised from the dead Jesus our Lord, who was put to death for our trespasses and raised for our justification" (4:23–25). The crucial phrase here is "to us who believe in him." Deliverance was effectuated only for those who believe in him, accept him. Manifestly Christ did not do away with sin as such because it is still present with us. He made it ineffectual for those who surrender to him and live in him.

3. The Quality of Salvation in Christ (5:1–21).

The observation above leads directly to the statement that "we have peace with God through our Lord Jesus Christ" (5:1). Doubtless the term peace is to be interpreted in the Hebraic sense of having regained the balance between God and man that had been drastically altered by sin. The quality of God's gift in Christ is expressed thus after the remark about Adam's sin: "For if many died through one man's trespass, much more have the grace of God and the free gift in the grace of that one man Jesus Christ abounded for many. . . . If, because of one man's trespass, death reigned through that one man, much more will those who receive the abundance of grace and the free gift of righteousness reign in life through the one man Jesus Christ" (5:15, 17). The superiority of grace for salvation from man's sin and trespasses is clearly expressed in the declaration that "where sin abounded, grace abounded all the more" (5:20). In a way this recalls another aspect of the exodus event. The determination of the Pharoah to keep Israel grew with a fever pitch as Moses and Aaron appealed to him "to let my people go." But the more adamant the Egyptian king became the more relentless was the pressure exerted by Yahweh. The Pharaoh's bondage was unto death; the grace of Yahweh exerted on behalf of his chosen people was for life and salvation. In the end the Pharaoh was hurled into the depths of the sea and his army with him. God's grace for life was more powerful than the arm of the Egyptian monarch. So too Christ had prevailed over the fierce power of sin and wrought deliverance for those who respond to him in faith, and that not for a single generation but for all mankind for all time to come.

4. The Character of God's Grace (6:1–23).

God's grace was available to all who believe in God through Christ. Sin had been nullified by God's mighty act in Christ for those who responded to and accepted his gift. But what was the character, of God's grace? In the exodus experience it spelled deliverance from Egyptian bondage to be followed by the ratification of God's promise to Abraham—the gift of the land wherein the people were free to live their lives in covenant relationship with him and one another. For Paul, God's grace was more. God's generosity to his delivered people—Christians—exceeded the mere act of the abrogation of bondage to sin; it conferred the power to keep free from its toils and involvements. In Christ the sinner had died to sin and had been resurrected to a new life. Henceforth he was no longer a slave to sin but a slave of righteousness (v. 20). In other words, he is a changed person. As E. F. Scott noted, Paul was "seeking to show the change effected by Christian faith is an essential and decisive one. When you become aware of the grace of God you are not merely influenced for a time in the right direction. You break away forever from the old life, and a new nature is born in you. As God has imparted his grace in one great act, so in the confession of Christ you perform your own act once for all. You die to sin and are alive to

God."[9] Because of what God had done necessity was laid upon the recipient of grace to exercise his willpower to lead a life consonant therewith. Enslavement to sin meant doing the works of sin; enslavement to righteousness meant doing the works of righteousness. Looking back from the vantage point of grace to that of slavery to sin revealed the shame characteristic of the former life in all its hideousness and ugliness, whose fruit is death. "But now that you have been set free from sin and have become slaves of God, the return you get is sanctification and its end, eternal life. For the wages of sin is death, but the free gift of God is eternal life in Christ Jesus our Lord" (vv. 22–23). To be covenanted to sin is to be dominated by it; to be covenanted to God through Christ is to be controlled by him and to be empowered to lead a life consonant with the life of Christ and enjoy the promised land of eternal bliss.

5. *The Higher and Lower Laws (7:1–25).*

Chapter 7 is perhaps the most enigmatic and tantalizing piece of argument in Romans. It deals with Paul's conception of the law and he begins with an illustration itself rather illogical. He equates the husband from whom the wife is freed after his death with the law. Since the law is dead the ones hitherto subject to it are free. But then Paul goes on to speak of the believer as dead to the law. With the coming of Christ, the law died. The believer baptized in the name of Christ has died to the law and been raised with Christ, i.e., he has renounced the old life and assumed the new life. But does that mean that the law was evil? By no means. If it had not been for the law Paul would not have known sin which would have remained dormant within him and continued working its insidious way with him. Before knowledge of the law he was perfectly happy (v. 8) and content. Then "when the commandment came, sin revived and I died; the very commandment which promised life proved to be death to me. For sin, finding opportunity in the commandment, deceived me and by it killed me. So the law is holy, and the commandment is holy and just and good" (9b–12). It was not the law that brought death to him. "It was sin, working death in me through what is good, in order that sin might be shown to be sin, and through the commandment might become sinful beyond measure" (13). Here is a striking statement of the two laws—the law of God and the law of sin and death. "I delight in the law of God, in my inmost self, but I see in my members another law of my mind and making me captive to the law of sin which dwells in my members" (22–23). Aware of this heart-rending tension he cried out, "O wretched man that I am! Who will deliver me from this body of death?" (24). Though he does not quote him, this was the same predicament voiced by Jeremiah in his conception of the new covenant that would be unlike the old covenant which was ruptured. The prophet was aware of the train of disobedience that plagued the nation and he had apparently come to the conclusion that more than a code written on stone was required to emancipate Israel from the clutches of transgression. Hence he announced Yahweh's determination: "I will put my torah within them, and will write it on their hearts" (31:33). In other words, with the law there will be an enabling power investing them with the ability to be truly his people. Jesus Christ was for Paul that power. The victory of the higher law over the lower came through him. In 1 Cor. 15:57 he exclaims, "thanks be to God, who gives us the victory through our Lord Jesus Christ."

6. The Function of the Spirit (8:1–27).

Up to this point the apostle has dealt with externals for the most part. Salvation which has been wrought for us has been achieved by the plainly evident act of the sacrifice of Christ. How then can it be appropriated by us? By faith! Yet something else seems to be needed if we are to become and remain the sons and daughters of God. "For the law of the Spirit of life in Christ Jesus has set me free from the law of sin and death" (2) so that I no longer live after the flesh. "Those who live according to the Spirit set their minds on the things of the Spirit" (5b). They have died to the flesh and the Spirit of God dwells in them: another way of saying that Christ lives in them, making their spirits alive because of righteousness (10). "If the Spirit of him who raised Jesus from the dead dwells in you, he who raised Christ Jesus from the dead will give life to your mortal bodies also through his Spirit which dwells in you" (11). Those in whom the Spirit of God dwells are the sons of God. While he is conscious that perfection has not yet been achieved, Paul looks forward in hope because he knows that the Spirit of God is working in man. The thrust of all creation is toward an "eager longing for the reveal-

71

ing of the sons of God" (19). And we ourselves "who have the birth certificate of the Spirit, groan inwardly as we wait for the adoption as sons, the redemption of our bodies" (23). All of this hope and longing is due to the workings of the Spirit who helps our weaknesses; it is he who intercedes for us because of ourselves we do not even know how to pray. The Spirit is God's gift (1 Thess. 4:8; Rom. 5:5) who dwells within us (1 Cor. 3:16). Just as we have been freed from the power of sin and death by God's grace, so we are empowered by the Spirit to live with Christ, or rather Christ lives in us.[10] It is the function of the Spirit to help us in our infirmities and so fulfill the law of Christ.

7. The Assurance of Salvation (8:28–39).

Paul's assurance of salvation for the believer recalls Moses' message of deliverance to the Hebrew slaves in Egypt. Neither Moses nor the elders were sure of Yahweh's determination and action until they were realized in the experience of salvation itself. That was not to be until the destruction of the Pharaoh and his host by the Reed Sea. Note again that Israel's deliverance was a pure act of God. "Do not fear," said Moses; "stand still and see how Yahweh is going to save you today. Though you see the Egyptians today, you will not see them again. Yahweh will contend for you; you have only to remain still" (Exod. 14:13b). The moment of salvation had come for Israel; henceforth they were assured that Yahweh had kept his promise to the fathers and had started them on the way to the promised land. Later on when, because of failure to maintain their response to the covenant, matters took a turn for the worse, the prophets looked forward to another intervention by God in the affairs of the people through a messiah, one anointed by him to deliver his people. Christians affirmed that Jesus Christ was their messiah. He had come as was manifest to all who believed, i.e., who accepted him as savior and Lord.

God had come in Christ to reconcile the world unto himself (2 Cor. 5:18 f). "He who did not spare his own Son but gave him up for us all, will he not also give us all things with him? . . . Is it Christ Jesus, who died, yes, who was raised from the dead, who is at the right hand of God who intercedes for us?" (Rom. 8:32, 34). What Paul and the other Christians of his time had encountered in Christ, living and crucified and resurrected; what

72

they had seen with their own eyes, touched with their hands, and felt in their lives confirmed without the shadow of doubt that in Christ their salvation was sure and certain. Henceforth they were convinced "that neither death, nor life, nor angels, nor principalities, nor things present, nor things to come, nor powers, nor height, nor depth, nor anything else in all creation will be able to separate us from the love of God in Christ Jesus our Lord" (Rom. 8:38b). The exodus signifies physical freedom for God's people; the Christ advent marks man's freedom for all men as spiritual beings.

C. COVENANTAL TERMINOLOGY IN ROMANS

Observations here are suggestive; they may reflect merely common language usages characteristic of the religious literature of both Jews and Christians. Nevertheless it is interesting to see how Romans is shot through with ideas and conceptions current in the religious documents of Israel, notably that referring to the exodus.

1. Salvation.

Exod. 14:13, Moses' statement requesting composure on the part of the troubled and impatient people on the shore of the Reed Sea, says, "see the salvation of Yahweh" (*yᵉšūʿat yahweh*). After the deliverance, in the great song of deliverance (15:2), they sang "he was my salvation" (*wayhi li lîšūʿāh*). Later on when Israel sinned and departed from their covenant stipulation, the Psalmist complained that they lost confidence in his salvation (*wᵉlʾo bāṭᵉḥū bîšūʿātō*) (Ps. 78:22b). In the Egyptian Hallel Psalm (118), the clause from Exod. 15:2 noted above is quoted twice (vv. 14, 21). The hymnal literature of Israel is permeated with the idea which undoubtedly derives from the exodus experience.

While the actual noun *sōtēriá* (salvation) occurs only five times in Romans[11] the idea is present everywhere. The verb *sódzō* (save) appears eight times in the first eleven chapters.[12] The reference to Moses and the Pharaoh in 9:15, 17 shows that the celebrated event of freedom from Egyptian bondage was not too far from the apostle's thoughts. The figure of the engrafting of wild olive branches into the cultivated olive tree (11:17 ff.) also points to the fact that somehow Paul conceived of redemption coming through Israel and that, in the last analysis, the fortunes of both

Jew and Gentile were in some way intertwined. Once again the only difference between the salvation of Israel from Egyptian bondage and that of all mankind in Christ is that the former is historical while the latter is historical-spiritual.

2. Freedom.

Closely related to the idea of salvation—perhaps even to be taken with it—is that of freedom. The watchword of the exodus is "Let my people go" (šallaḥ) (Exod. 5:1; 4:23; 7:16; 8:1, 20; 9:1, 13; 10:3)—really send my people away, from bondage and slavery, that they may "serve" me. God's mighty hand freed his people from enslavement for the ostensible purpose of serving him and later enjoying his gift of a land flowing with milk and honey.

According to Paul, men are enslaved to and in bondage to sin. While we were yet helpless, in hopeless bondage to sin, Christ died for us (5:6) so that "we might no longer be enslaved to sin." "Who will deliver me from this body of death?" (7:24). "The law of the Spirit of life in Christ Jesus has set me free from the law of sin and death" (8:2). Just as Israel groaned under the bondage of Egypt, so the whole creation has been groaning in travail (8:22) and has now been "set free from its bondage to decay and obtain the glorious liberty of the children of God" (8:21). We have been enslaved to sin (6:6) but have now been freed from sin to become slaves of righteousness (6:18). In a great paean of exultation Paul exclaims: "But now that you have been set free from sin and have become slaves of God, the return you get is sanctification and its end, eternal life" (6:22). One must wonder if the backdrop to such ideas and language is not that matchless deliverance of Israel from slavery! The historical experience of Israel has been theologized and made more profound and more widely applicable. What was an event in history has been transmuted into a cosmic, spiritual transaction.

3. God's Mercy or Steadfast Love (ḥesed).

It is well-known that ḥesed is a covenant term[13] and is difficult to translate. But it is applied generally to a relationship within the covenant so that God's ḥesed expresses devotion, loyalty to his people. Exod. 15:13 speaks of Yahweh leading his redeemed people in his ḥesed, i.e., because of covenant devotion in the fulfillment of his promise to the fathers. Hosea charges that *kî* *'ēn-ᵉmeth wᵉ'ēn ḥesed wᵉda'at 'ᵉlōhîm bā'āreṣ* (there is no faithfulness and no *ḥesed* and no knowledge of God in the land) (4:1) and affirms of Yahweh *kî ḥesed ḥāphaṣti wᵉl'ō-zebaḥ* (for *ḥesed* I delight in and not sacrifice) (6:6). Micah declares that Yahweh *'ahᵃbath ḥesed* (loves *ḥesed*) (6:8).

Now while it is generally said that for Paul there was no longer evident *ḥesed* because the covenant had been irrevocably fractured so that God had to begin anew, it may equally well be stated that the concept is not wholly absent from his mind. He uses *eleein, éleos* (to show mercy, pity) a number of times, words used overwhelmingly in LXX to render *ḥesed,* but they seem to have no covenant significance in the context of the epistle. Paul generally employs *cháris* (favor, grace) (ca. 16 times), which has a different flavor than *ḥesed*; it corresponds to the Hebrew *ḥēn*. In Rom. 3:12, quoting LXX of Ps. 13:1 (Heb. and English = 14:1), the word *chrēstótēs* (goodness) is used to render the Heb. *ṭôb*. Now the same word is found also in 11:22 where a condition is attached to God's kindness: "'God's kindness to you, provided you remain in his kindness; otherwise you too will be cut off." God's deliverance from sin and death demands a faith response as we shall see, i.e., *ḥesed* on the part of the recipients of God's grace.

4. God's Grace.

In the Old Testament the verb *ḥānan* (to show favor) "would seem to bestow a kindness which could not have been claimed, used either of God or men."[14] Much the same can be predicated of the noun *ḥēn* (grace, favor). Paul nowhere quotes a text from the Old Testament to support any of his arguments though he certainly has the idea which, as noted above, he expressed by the word *cháris*. He naturally hits upon the concept by virtue of his belief that God's covenant with man has been broken so that he no longer has any claim upon God. What God does is pure grace, and rests upon his free choice. In Rom. 9:15, Exod. 33:19 is cited *wᵉḥannōthî 'et-ᵃšer 'ahon—eleéso òn àn eleó* (i.e., I will bestow favor upon whom I bestow favor). In both contexts the reference is to the free, unbound act of God, who chooses to grant favor to whomsoever he will. But that very decision establishes a relationship based on good will or love which issues in response, acceptance. It is the first step in a grace-faith relationship and, though not covenantal in itself, the initial move toward such an affiliation.

5. The Commandments.

Another consideration relative to Paul's religious background is his direct and indirect reference to the commandments. Surely his frequent condemnation of the Jewish use of the law provides some indication of what he had in mind and perhaps the milieu out of which it came. That he is still in awe of the torah may be seen from his condemnation of images (1:23), the list of evils (1:29b) among which are covetousness, murder, deceit, disobedience to parents, etc., the illustration in one of the arguments in support of his view of the law by referring to the commandments against adultery and idols (2:22, 23), and especially the bit of autobiography that involved his nemesis before the commandment against coveting (7:7 ff.).

In addition there is rather frequent mention of obedience—"obedience to the faith" (1:5). There is no equivocation in exhortation to well-doing: "For he (God) will render to every man according to his works: to those who by patience in well-doing seek for glory and honor and immortality, he will give eternal life; but for those who are factious and do not obey the truth, but obey wickedness, there will be wrath and fury" (2:6–8). Again, Paul asserts that "by one man's disobedience many were made sinners" and "by one man's obedience many will be made righteous" (5:18). Here the whole matter of the divine-human relationship is removed from the level of the code and referred to that of the personal. The same subject is continued in 6:16 ff.: "Do you not know that if you yield yourselves to any one as obedient slaves, you are slaves of the one whom you obey, either of sin, which leads to death, or of obedience, which leads to righteousness? But thanks be to God, that you who were once slaves of sin have become obedient from the heart to the standard of teaching to which you were committed, and, having been set free from sin, have become slaves of righteousness."

Ethical dicta interspersing the theological arguments are quite prominent. This may be seen from the apostle's bitter outburst against homosexuality in 1:26–27 and the catalogue of aberrations in 1:28–32; or this injunction: "Do not yield your members to sin as instruments of wickedness, but yield yourselves to God as instruments of righteousness" (6:13). Others along the same line could be cited.

6. The Righteousness of God.

This expression occurs six times in Romans (1:17; 3:21, 22, 25, 26; 10:3) and in 2 Cor. 5:21 and Phil. 3:9. Its meaning, noted above, has been the subject of a great deal of discussion.[15] In the sense used here "Righteousness is a matter of man's relationship to God, not an ethical state."[16] C. H. Dodd, commenting on Rom. 1:17, writes, "The life and death of Jesus Christ, His resurrection, and the creation of the Church through His Spirit, constitute a decisive Act of God, an objective revelation of His righteousness."[17] Thus the righteousness of God is salvific in nature and not forensic. This conception is present also in the Old Testament as has been shown by Father John J. Scullion[18] who reports on a study of $s^e d\bar{a}q\bar{a}h$-$sedeq$ by J. P. Justesen.[19] Justesen found that out of 117 occurrences of $sedeq$, 67 (57%) are connected with law; of the 115 occurrences of $s^e d\bar{a}q\bar{a}h$ only 45 (29%) are so connected. In the usages of the $sedeq$ group in II Isaiah, Psalms, and Judges the meaning approximates that of "save," "saving," "salvation." In summary he concludes that "its central thrust is to describe a judicial and soteriological process of judging, acquitting and saving. When applied to the initiator of such action it assumes the concepts of merciful, compassionate, benevolent, and good."[20] James Muilenburg writes of the covenantal significance of the term in Isa. 61:10.[21] If, as the commentators assert for the most part, the righteousness of God signifies his gift of salvation, there would seem to be a rather close relation with the exodus event which likewise points to Yahweh's salvation. We cannot, however, be sure whether that event was in Paul's mind though the cumulative evidence seems suggestive, to say the least.

Incidentally, the same idea appears in the Qumran literature. A few quotations will illustrate the point.

> To God I will say, my righteousness,
> And to the Most High, the Creator of my goodness. IQS 10:11b.

> By his righteousness he has wiped out my transgression. IQS 11:3.

> From the source of his righteousness is my justification. IQS 11:5.

On that which is forever my eyes gazed . . .
the source of righteousness and the storehouse of power. IQS
11:5 ff.

And I, if I stumble the steadfast love of God is my eternal
salvation,
And if I totter in fleshly iniquity my justification will be in
eternal righteousness of God. IQS 11:11b.

By his righteousness he will cleanse me
of the filth of man and of the sins of mankind. IQS 11:14b.

For I lean on your steadfast loves
and the multitude of your compassions.
For you will forgive iniquity
and purify man of guilt through your righteousness.
. . . .
I will take courage in your covenant. IQH 4:37 ff.

D. THE BROADER PATTERN OF ROMANS

We have drawn attention, at the beginning of this chapter, to
the gospel-torah pattern of the exodus event, the New Testament,
and especially Romans. There the apostle deals with the righteousness of God, i.e., his salvation victory, embodied in the life,
death, and resurrection of Jesus Christ and its availability to all
who believe in him. God acted out of sheer grace to provide for
man's deliverance from sin and consequent death, just as he had
for Israel's freedom from physical slavery and bondage. No prior
act of sacrifice occurs in conjunction with the exodus act. Israel
had nothing to give at the time. The offer of salvation, grace—
full though it may be—is of no value unless it is appropriated.
Israel had to say 'yes' to Yahweh, i.e., accept the offer of liberation, respond to his gift of emancipation, by becoming his slave
or servant. The plea of Moses to the Pharaoh was, "Release my
people that they may hold a feast to me in the desert" (Exod.
5:1)—the formula Yahweh had commanded him to speak. But
Israel had to have the desire to accept liberation; presumably
they did because they previously cried unto Yahweh by virtue of
their harsh treatment at the hands of the Egyptians. After the
series of steps from Goshen to Sinai with all their vicissitudes,
Yahweh announced his covenant with his delivered people at
the place where they were holding festival to him—I will be your
God and you will be my people. Yahweh's grace did not cease

with release from Egyptian servitude; it manifested itself further in the gift of torah, i.e., direction for remaining free from further and more devasting enslavement and the living of lives of gratitude for Yahweh's unremitting loyalty and devotion to his chosen people.

Now Romans follows the same general model. The portion of the epistle dealt with above had as its theme the gospel as "the power of God for salvation to everyone who has faith." "In it the righteousness of God is revealed," i.e., the salvific act of God is made plain for everyone to see. Then Paul goes on to show how that is so as it applies to people caught in the intricate toils of sin who are impotent to set themselves free. God has done that in Jesus Christ for everyone who responds in faith, both Jew and Greek. The old man had perished and the new man in Christ was born. By the aid of the spirit he was made alive in Christ in whom he now lived.

What kind of life was it to be? Paul tells us in no uncertain terms what the quality of that life is in chapters 12 to 15. "*Therefore* I call upon you, brothers, by the mercies of God to present yourselves as a living sacrifice to God which is your rightful worship" (12:1). "Do not," he goes on, "be conformed to this world but be transformed by the renewal of your mind, that you may prove by the test (*dokimadzō*) what is the will of God, what is good and well-pleasing and perfect" (12:2). The crucial word in these verses, indeed for the whole section, is the inferential particle *oun* (therefore) which "signifies that something follows from what precedes."[22] Because of God's saving act in Christ to which the believer is committed, it follows that he (the believer) is a new creation whose guidelines Paul now sets forth—somewhat like those laid down in the torah. The one who has accepted Christ's salvation is no longer his own; he is Christ's. "You are my people," said Yahweh to redeemed Israel. And Paul says elsewhere (1 Cor. 6:19–20; 7:23), "You are not your own; you were bought with a price."

Details of what is expected of one who is Christ's are then spelled out rather carefully. (1) He must recognize his position as a servant of Christ; he must not be conceited or think of himself too highly, remembering always that he is just one member of the body of Christ (12:3–5). (2) Nevertheless he must use cheerfully whatever gifts have been allotted to him in the service of the whole community (12:6–8). (3) He must love sincerely the brotherhood so that it may experience the warmth of mutual affection, shun evil, and hold fast to what is good (12:9–10). (4) He must serve the Lord with unwavering energy and fervor of spirit, joyful in hope, standing firm in times of adversity, and be persistent in prayer (12:11–12). (5) He must be charitable, blessing rather than cursing persecutors, and really be all things to all men. Furthermore he must disclaim special privilege (12:13–16). (6) He must not seek revenge, and strive to live peacefully with all men (12:17–21). (7) He must not be slack in the performance of his civic duties, pay his taxes, and be guided by the Levitical principle (Lev. 19:18) of loving his neighbors as himself (13:1–10). (8) Because the parousia is at hand, he must "cast off the works of darkness and put on the armor of light," conduct himself becomingly and not revel in drunkenness, and abstain from debauchery, licentiousness, quarreling and jealousy (13:11–14). (9) He must not get involved in senseless cultic arguments that might cause a brother to stumble. Rather let him pursue the things that make for peace and the edification of the common life (14:1–15:6). (10) In short, he must be a Christ to his fellows, i.e., "accept one another as Christ accepted us" (NEB, 15:7) (15:7–13).[23]

NOTES

1. *The Covenant Formulary: In Old Testament, Jewish, and Early Christian Writings,* trans. David E. Green. (Philadelphia: Fortress Press, 1971), p. xiii. See further his Synopsis, p. 179; F. C. Fensham, "The Covenant as giving Expression to the Relationship Between Old and New Testament," *Tyndale Bulletin* 22 (1971): 82–94; R. Nixon, "New Wine in Old Wine-Skins: VII. Exodus," *The Expository Times* 85 (Dec. 1973): 72–75 and references cited there; and Robert Nixon, *The Exodus in the New Testament* (London: Tyndale Press, 1963); W. D. Davies, "The Moral Teaching in the Early Church" in *The Use of the Old Testament in the New and Other Essays: Studies in Honor of William Franklin Stinespring,* ed. J. M. Efird (Durham, N.C.: Duke University Press, 1972), pp. 311 ff., with bibliography.

2. *An Introduction to the New Testament* (Chicago: University of Chicago Press, 1937), pp. 73–84.

3. *Ibid.,* p. 77.

4. *Ibid.,* p. 82.

5. E.g., W. Pauck, *Luther: Lectures on Romans,* Library of Christian Classics, vol. 15 (Philadelphia: Westminster Press, 1961). Luther devotes 99 of 419 pp. to this section. K. Barth, *The Epistle to the Romans,* trans. of 6th ed. by E. C. Hoskyns (London: Oxford University Press, 5th impression, 1960) has 113 of 537 pp.: M.-J. Lagrange, *Saint Paul,*

Epitre aux Romains (Paris: Gabalda, 1950), 71 of 361 pp.; A. Nygren, *Commentary on Romans*, trans. C. C. Rasmussen (Philadelphia: Muhlenberg Press, 1949), 42 of 457 pp.; W. Sanday and A. C. Headlam, *The Epistle to the Romans* (ICC) (New York: Scribner, 14th ed. 1913), 66 of 416 pp.; W. Luther, *The Letter to the Romans,* trans. K. Schoenenberger (Richmond: John Knox Press, 1961), 53 of 212 pp.; O. Michel, *Der Brief an die Römer* (Göttingen: Vandenhoeck & Ruprecht, 12th ed. 1963), 86 of 374 pp.

6. Cf. C. H. Dodd, *The Gospel and Law* (New York: Columbia University Press, 1961), esp. p. 78 f.; James Moffatt, *Grace in the New Testament* (New York: Ray Long & Richard R. Smith, 1932), pp. 181 ff.

7. Cf. the satires of Persius (A.D. 34–62) and Juvenal (A.D. 1/2 century).

8. Cf. reference cited in note 32 of preceding chapter. Cf. M. Black, *Romans*, New Century Bible (Greenwood, S.C.: Attic Press, 1973), p. 44 f.; O. Michel, *Der Brief an die Römer* (Göttingen: Vandenhoeck & Ruprecht, 1963), p. 53 f.; F. J Leenhardt, *The Epistle to the Romans* (London: Lutterworth Press, 1961), pp. 49–58. For a rabbinic assessment of Paul's argument see Eugene Mihaly, "A Rabbinic Defense of the Election of Israel" in *Hebrew Union College Annual,* vol. 35 (Cincinnati, 1964), pp. 103–143.

9. *Paul's Epistle to the Romans* (London: SCM Press, 1947), p. 45. The writer is greatly indebted to this stimulating and penetrating study for much of the direction of his thought in this chapter.

10. See Moffatt, *op. cit.,* pp. 182 ff.

11. 1:16; 10:1, 10; 11:11; 13:11.

12. 5:9, 10; 8:24; 9:27; 10:9, 13; 11:14, 26.

13. See N. H. Snaith, *The Distinctive Ideas of the Old Testament* (London: Epworth Press, 1944), pp. 94–130, and N. Glueck, *Das Wort hesed* (Giessen: Töpelmann, 1927), esp. chap. 3 on *hesed* as a way of divine attitude or conduct.

14. W. F. Lofthouse, "Hen and Hesed in the Old Testament," *ZAW,* 51 (1933): 29, 33: "For *hesed* is not used indiscriminately, where any kind of favor is desired, but only where there is some recognized tie or claim. It is indeed the very opposite of *hēn,* which is in place just where there is no tie or claim."

15. Cf. H. Lietzmann, *An die Römer: HzNT,* 8 (Tübingen: J. C. B. Mohr [Paul Siebeck], 3d ed., 1928): 30–31, 48–51, and esp. the excursus on p. 95.

16. P. J. Achtemeier in *IDB* (New York-Nashville: Abingdon Press, 1962), 4:95.

17. *The Epistle of Paul to the Romans*: The Moffatt Commentary (New York: Harpers, 1932), p. 13. So also E. Lohmeyer, *Die Briefe an die Philipper, an die Kolosser und an Philemon* (Göttingen: Vandenhoeck & Ruprecht, 1930), p. 137; G. Bornkamm, *Das Ende des Gesetzes: Gesammelte Aufsätze I* (Munich: Kaiser Verlag, 1961) who says (p. 9), that righteousness of God is "realization of the salvation event that God has shown to the world in Jesus Christ and that actualizes itself in the performance of the gospel"; and G. A. F. Knight, *Law and Grace* (London: SCM Press, 1962), chaps. 9 and 10.

18. See note 7.

19. "On the meaning of SADAQ," *Andrews University Seminary Studies* (Michigan), 2 (1964): 53–61.

20. *Ibid.*, p. 60 f.

21. "The Book of Isaiah: Chapters 40–66," *The Interpreter's Bible* (New York-Nashville: Abingdon Press, 1956), 5:714.

22. H. W. Smyth, *A Greek Grammar for Colleges* (New York: American Book Company, 1920), 2964. Cf Latin *itaque*, Syriac *hakil* = thus, therefore, accordingly.

23. The whole of Rom. 12:1–15:13 has remarkable similarities to IQS 10:5–11:23. For a comparison between some vv. of Rom. 12–14 and Matthew see W. D. Davies, *op. cit.* (note 1), pp. 324–327.

Conclusion

The pattern of grace-torah has been discussed in four areas of the Bible: first in the Exodus-Sinai event, then the order in the early prophets, in Deuteronomy and the later prophets, and finally the salvation-torah design in Romans.

In chapter I we noted that in the Old Testament everything appears to be based on either God's choice of Abraham with the latter's response or the Exodus-Sinai archetype, mostly the latter. God heard the lament of his people, because of their oppression in Egypt and delivered them by a mighty hand and outstretched arm. He responded to their further cries at their lack of water and food and saved them at the Reed Sea by destroying the Pharaoh and his host. At Sinai he gave them his covenant in which he pledged himself to be their God.[1] In another superlative act of grace he gave them his torah wherein he provided them with direction as to how to remain in covenant relationship with him, how to respond to his salvation, how to remain free from re-enslavement to other nations, idols, and themselves. In other words Yahweh told them how to keep saved! The torah was thus not an instrument of salvation[2] —that had already taken place—but a characterization of life-principles reflecting the state or quality of the saved people, a living thank offering to the God of their salvation.

In a recent study, Peter Weimar[3] shows how the priestly writers utilized the old traditions of the exodus and succeeding events to instruct and encourage the Jews of the early post-exilic period. P reworked an earlier tradition accentuating the oppression of Israel in Egypt, together with the announcement of deliverance of the erstwhile slaves by Yahweh, to reassert the validity of his grace for a new historical situation. The emphasis of P falls not only on deliverance as such but more on that of leading Israel into the land Yahweh had promised and given to his people. Sections of the patriarchal history were combined with the three-fold tradition of exodus, Sinai, and the gift of the land. It is significant that stress is laid on the contest between Yahweh/Moses and Pharaoh/the gods of Egypt which demonstrated Yahweh's power and glory; the Egyptians knew by his mighty acts that Yahweh was Lord of history. Now the exiles had lost interest in the land, as may be seen from the difficulties encountered with the rather affluent Jews[4] by the leaders of the *gôlāh,* and doubted the power and concern of Yahweh for them. Hence, following the preachments of the Second Isaiah, the authors of P endeavored to arouse the early *gôlāh* and revive the faith of the Jews in Babylon who remained indifferent to the summons to return to Judah and Jerusalem. They proclaimed hope in an atmosphere of despair. Yahweh, the Lord of history, will remain true to his promise which was fulfilled in the past and will be fulfilled again by his gift of grace—the gift of deliverance and restoration in the land. In other words, the Lord of history will continue to be gracious to his people through all time.

Chapters II and III investigated, in a very general way, covenantal patterns and thought in the early and late prophetic periods. Covenantal language and concepts persist in both periods. The early prophets charge the nation with ingratitude because there was "no fidelity, no (covenant) loyalty, no knowledge (real acquaintance) of God in the land" (Hos. 4:1). Judgment, though conceived in contemporary terms, was really self-destruction through ingratitude displayed in the flouting of the God's torah. The final attempt to restore the covenant relationship came in the Deuteronomic reformation whose aim was to save the nation, or rather for the nation to avoid suicide, by the imposition of cultic and other reforms. The failure of such a course is evident from the history of Judah in 597 B.C. and 587 B.C. as Jeremiah had foreseen. The covenant was a matter of the heart, not the cultus. The nation would have to be saved again from "Egypt," then perhaps in a newly experienced deliverance would respond in a torah of gratitude. That was the hope of II Isaiah and the aim of the post-exilic prophets, though the situation in those difficult times required peculiar exhortations and recommendations.

In the last chapter we have taken an overall look at the order followed by St. Paul in Romans and discovered that a similar pattern is followed there. We have seen the possibility of covenantal terminology in the so-called doctrinal portion of the letter but more significant and impressive is the fact that it stands where

CONCLUSION

it does. It describes and argues the point of the righteousness-salvation of God in Jesus Christ through whom the world has been saved. Salvation is a gift, God's grace to mankind. No conditions were attached to God's act. Only faith was necessary to appropriate it. But then Paul goes on to point out how saved men ought to conduct themselves with reference to the community and the world. Such conduct of the believer demonstrated that he was really in Christ, a slave of his and no longer his own. It would be a life of thanksgiving for God's gracious gift of both salvation and direction.[5]

Therefore

I will choose what he will teach me,
And I will be satisfied however he judges me.
IQS 10:12 f.

NOTES

1. Cf. G. A. F. Knight, *Law and Grace* (London: SCM Press, 1962), p. 30.
2. See G. F. Moore, *Judaism* (Cambridge: Harvard University Press, 1927), 2:95.
3. *Untersuchungen zur priesterschriftlichen Exodusgeschichte.* Wurzburg: Echter Verlag, 1973. Esp. pp. 169–172, 246–252.
4. See W. F. Albright, *The Biblical Period from Abraham to Ezra* (New York: Harper Torchbooks, 1963), p. 87; J. M. Myers, *The World of the Restoration* (Englewood Cliffs, N.J.: Prentice-Hall, 1968), pp. 49, 53.
5. If there is no experience and manifestation of the torah in one's daily life in relation to his covenant brothers, he cannot be said to stand in the covenant relationship. Dr. James D. G. Dunn, "Rediscovering the Spirit" (*The Expository Times*, vol. 74, Oct. 1972, p. 8), believes that the "presence or absence of the Spirit in a man's (or community's) life was directly knowable and perceptible—not the Spirit as such, of course, but his presence." In Rom. 8:9, Paul declares, "Any one who does not have the spirit of Christ does not belong to him." To be in Christ is to be imbued with the Spirit whose fruit is "love, joy, peace, patience, kindness, goodness, faithfulness, gentleness, self-control" (Gal. 5:23). "If any one is in Christ he is a new creation" (2 Cor. 5:17). Former things have passed away and the new life in a world of promise has been born for all to see. "By their fruits shall you know them," said the Lord of life (Matt. 7:16). Walter Eichrodt has observed, in connection with Ezek. 18:31, that "The truth is rather that here, just as in the New Testament, the imperative of the exhortation is a response to the indicative of God's saving action; God's gift of salvation does not leave man alone, but calls upon him for a response to God's offer, to enter upon the new potentiality of life that has been granted him. Paul requires of believers nothing less than transformation by the renewing of their mind (Rom. 12:2), precisely because he acknowledges the all-sufficiency of the grace of God." *Ezekiel* (Philadelphia: Westminster Press, 1970), p. 246. See further, W. D. Davies, "The Relevance of the Moral Teaching of the Early Church" in *Neotestamentica et Semitica:*

85

Studies in honour of Principal Matthew Black, ed. E. E. Ellis and M. Wilcox (Edinburgh: T. & T. Clark, 1969), pp. 30–49, esp. p. 43; and B. O. Reicke, "The New Testament Conception of Reward" in *Aux sources de la tradition Chrétienne: Mélanges offerts à Maurice Goguel* (Paris: Delachaux et Niestlé, 1950), pp. 195–206.